AMERICAN HORTICULTURAL SOCIETY
PRACTICAL GUIDES

PERENNIALS

AMERICAN HORTICULTURAL SOCIETY
PRACTICAL GUIDES

PERENNIALS

RAY EDWARDS

DK PUBLISHING, INC.
www.dk.com

A DK PUBLISHING BOOK
www.dk.com

PROJECT EDITOR Cangy Venables
ART EDITOR Margherita Gianni

SERIES EDITOR Pamela Brown
SERIES ART EDITOR Stephen Josland
US EDITOR Ray Rogers

MANAGING EDITOR Louise Abbott
MANAGING ART EDITOR Lee Griffiths

DTP DESIGNER Matthew Greenfield

PRODUCTION MANAGER Patricia Harrington

First American Edition, 1999
4 6 8 10 9 7 5 3

Published in the United States by
DK Publishing, Inc., 95 Madison Avenue, New York, New York 10016

Copyright © 1999
Dorling Kindersley Limited, London

Library of Congress Cataloging-in-Publication Data

Perennials. -- 1st American ed.
    p.   cm.   -- (AHS practical guides)
  Includes index.
  ISBN 0–7894–4151–9 (alk. paper)
  1. Perennials. I. DK Publishing, Inc. II. Series.
SB434.P4733 1999
635.9'32--dc21   98–41493
                                                CIP

Reproduced by Colourscan, Singapore
Printed and bound by Star Standard Industries, Singapore

CONTENTS

PERENNIALS IN THE GARDEN 7

What are perennials, and why are they so versatile?
Choosing perennials to suit your garden, sustaining
interest throughout the year, and designing with color.

PLANTING PLANS FOR PERENNIALS 27

TRADITIONAL BORDER STYLE 27
NATURALISTIC PLANTING 33
PLANTING IN SHADE 37
PLANTING IN MOIST GROUND 41
PERENNIALS IN CONTAINERS 45

LOOKING AFTER PERENNIALS 49

How to prepare the soil, give your plants a good start,
care for them throughout the year, and raise new plants
from seed, from cuttings, and by division.

RECOMMENDED PERENNIALS 65

Descriptions and cultivation tips for a wide range of
perennials for both flowering and foliage interest to suit
any garden site, soil, and style.

Index 78
Acknowledgments 80

PERENNIALS IN THE GARDEN

WHAT IS A PERENNIAL?

TAKEN LITERALLY, THE TERM "perennial," as used in botany, embraces all plants that produce vegetative growth for at least three years – that is, anything from a daisy up to a tree. However, when it is applied to garden plants, it usually refers to herbaceous plants: those with growth that does not become woody, except perhaps around the base, or "crown," of the plant as it matures.

HARDINESS

Perennials are able to survive the local weather conditions, especially the lowest winter temperatures, without protection. As a group, they are some of the most valuable plants to the gardener. Some are best replaced after three or four years in favor of young, fresh specimens; others remain vigorous for 30 years or more. Most cope with severe weather by dying back in autumn, the crown and roots remaining dormant below ground until the temperature rises again in spring. Some perennials are described as evergreen, but in fact are not strictly so; their leaves and stems are simply tough enough to remain intact in winter. They are replaced by fresh growth in spring, when most gardeners prefer to trim off the previous year's growth, which, although it may have survived, has generally become tattered by the physical effects of weathering: for example, freezing and thawing of the tissues, and by snow, sun, and wind.

► CENTER STAGE
In small planting areas, groups of perennials can create tapestries of flowers and foliage.

◄ LASTING SHOW
Year after year, perennials can contribute color and texture to every garden, whatever the site and soil conditions.

Most perennials are not difficult to grow and look after, and there is an enormous variety to choose from. The majority will adapt to less than perfect conditions; some will positively thrive in the most "problematic" of sites, such as a shady corner or in an area with permanently moist soil. They come in an enormous range of sizes, colors, textures, and shapes, making it possible to create all kinds of designs and effects that will suit even the smallest space. Their diversity makes them ideal for every style of garden, and there are many that are just as at home in containers as in the open ground.

CHOOSING PERENNIALS

The choice of perennials is so great that you could fill the largest of gardens with nothing else, yet still enjoy almost 12 months of interest (see pp.12–19). Most gardeners are drawn to perennials for their huge range of flower forms and colors, but

STRIKING DESIGNS
Theme borders need careful planning and siting, but the results can be dramatic. This bed, composed mainly of asters, penstemons, and chrysanthemums, glows with color in late summer.

remember that interest comes from foliage, too; leaves and grasses can look extremely effective, especially with a dusting of snow on dry stems and seedheads.

GROUPING PLANTS TOGETHER

In most gardens, perennials are simply one element among other types of plants (see p.10). But planting designs consisting solely

> The sheer diversity of perennials makes them ideal for any garden style

of perennials, carefully chosen to grow well together, can be beautiful and long-lasting. Later in this book you will find a number of planting plans that suggest groupings for various sites and in various styles; all are designed using plants that will, hopefully, be readily available, but a good garden center will be able to suggest alternatives, or you may prefer to choose from the Recommended Perennials at the back of the book. Notes, and even the roughest plan of what you think you can

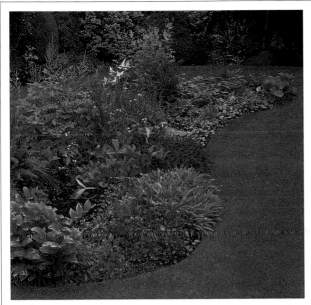

◀ ISLAND LIFE
*Use perennials of different
heights to create a herbaceous
landscape in island beds.*

▼ BRIGHT IDEA
*Pots filled with variegated
grasses can be used to
brighten up a dull corner.*

achieve in the space and on the site and soil available, will help enormously when buying plants. In small gardens this is particularly important.

PLANTING STYLES AND IDEAS

Few sights are finer than a traditional, well-filled herbaceous border (*see p.27*), especially when set against a formal clipped hedge or attractive wall or fence. A more informal look can be achieved by allowing cottage garden or naturalistic plantings (*see p.33*) to break out of border constraints and spill over paths and lawns. Low-growing, creeping, herbaceous perennials give interest to dull expanses of paving and soften the edges of brick, gravel, or concrete paths. An island bed with an informal curving outline is another option.

Lots of perennials have fragrant flowers, and some have aromatic foliage: position these where you can enjoy their scent. Many make good cutting plants, yielding flowers for the home. Others grow well in containers, easy to place where you can appreciate them at close quarters: on the patio, for instance, or close to a door.

BREAK FROM THE BORDER
*Bleak expanses of gravel, concrete, or paving
may be softened by allowing low-growing
perennials to spill out from borders.*

MIXED PLANTINGS

OVER THE PAST CENTURY, shrinking garden size has had an effect on the way perennials are used. Nowadays, few people possess a garden large enough to incorporate large, traditional borders devoted entirely to herbaceous perennials. Consequently, these plants are more likely to be interspersed among shrubs, bulbs, and annuals to create mixed plantings, which can be planned in a formal style but often tend more to what romantics term a "cottage garden."

CREATING STRUCTURAL INTEREST

Integrated planting increases the height range in borders, extends seasonal interest, and is usually much less labor intensive than a design devoted solely to herbaceous plants. Existing beds and borders may already have a complement of shrubs, which will retain their shape, and sometimes their leaves, all year. Shallow-rooting perennials that are not too greedy, such as geraniums, make wonderful "skirts" for the bare lower stems of roses.

SHELTER AND HEIGHT
Walls and fences provide useful sheltered sites for warmth-loving perennials and provide support for a backdrop of climbing plants.

In established gardens, borders may be overshadowed by woody plants. Partial shade suits many herbaceous perennials; dense shade, however, will seriously restrict your choice, so consider removing or thinning some old trees and shrubs. There's usually no harm in politely asking neighbors if they would consider thinning theirs.

If starting a garden from scratch, place trees and shrubs first, with taller ones at the back and lower ones at the front. These can also be used as hosts for climbing plants; other freestanding climber supports, such as poles or tripods, can help enormously by providing height in exposed beds, where tall perennials might suffer from wind damage.

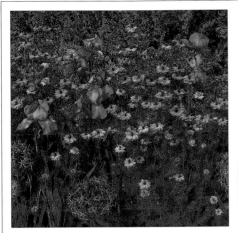

◄ FILLING OUT THE BORDER
*Annuals, such as these blue nigellas, make
excellent fillers for any gaps that appear
between perennials (here iris and alliums), and
they frequently self-seed themselves.*

▼ THEMED MIXED PLANTING
*Group plants of different types that enjoy
similar conditions: this hot and sunny spot
contains gladioli and shrubby cistus with
felted verbascums and feathery crambe.*

ANNUALS AND BULBS

Lightweight, annual climbers such as
canary creeper (*Tropaeolum peregrinum*)
can be planted to twine among robust
perennials. Annuals mature quickly and can
usually be sown directly where they are to
flower, either in the early autumn or spring.

Sow annuals as gap fillers while perennials are still small

They make excellent gap fillers while
perennials mature. They will sometimes
self-seed, reappearing the following year:
you can weed them out or keep them,
depending on where they are growing.

Spring bulbs can be used to create
superb combinations, not only with early-
flowering perennials but with the fresh
colors and textures of their newly emerging
foliage. The bulbs' leaves will die down to
yield the stage to summer plants. Bedding
plants, and containers full of late spring-
and summer-flowering bulbs such as lilies,
also make very effective stopgaps, useful
when unexpected casualties occur or for
covering bare areas of ground where
foliage from spring-flowering bulbs has
been cleared away.

PERENNIALS FOR SPRING

TRADITIONALLY, PERENNIALS ARE USED to give their finest display in summer, yet there are plenty that are valuable for spring interest. One of the best reasons for planning planting groups carefully is to ensure that there are plants good to look at at all times of year spread evenly throughout the design, complementing other types of plants such as bulbs and shrubs.

A RENEWAL OF GROWTH

Hellebores are the first perennials to flower in the year. The glistening white flowers of Christmas rose *(Helleborus niger)* appear in late winter, followed by the Lenten rose *(Helleborus orientalis)* in a medley of white, pink, and purple shades, with many of the flowers delicately spotted and splashed on the inside.

As winter gives way to spring, the pace of growth accelerates. T m away old, scruffy foliage of perennials that has persisted through winter to let all the beauty of the young growth shine through. Most early-flowering herbaceous perennials are low-growing, so position them at the front of beds and borders. Plant them in

groups to make substantial clumps, with interplantings of early spring bulbs; later, the fading bulb leaves will be hidden as the plants grow. In early spring, blue and white-flowered lungworts *(Pulmonaria)* are early-flowering favorites, along with the taller growing Siberian forget-me-nots *(Brunnera)*. Many of the former have attractive silver-splashed and spotted foliage, while several variegated forms of the latter are ideal for brightening up shadier spots in the border. Cool, fresh color combinations can be achieved by mixing them with small spring bulbs such as white snowdrops and blue scillas and grape hyacinths. For warmth, yellow and cream-colored globeflowers *(Trollius)*

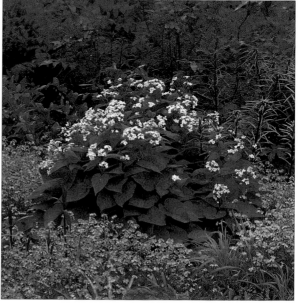

▶ FRESH FLOWER CLUMPS
A clump of brunnera holds court at the front of the spring border, surrounded by crowds of admiring scillas.

▼ FIRST TO BLOOM
Creamy hellebores and blue pulmonarias signal the return of spring to plantings of perennials.

NEW GROWTH
The fresh, new foliage of perennials emerging in spring – here hostas, stachys, tanacetum, and lupines – makes a lovely textural foil for flowering bulbs such as these tulips, their white purity echoed in the leaf margins of the variegated hosta.

quickly follow, along with the pink and crimson hues of bergenia flowers, many still resplendent in coppery winter foliage.

By late spring borders are swinging into color, much of it provided by old-fashioned favorites including leopard's bane (*Doronicum*), columbines (*Aquilegia*), and foam flower (*Tiarella*). If you are hoping that some perennials will have self-seeded, be careful on early weeding forays: while some plants, including columbines, are quite distinctive from an early age, others,

---

Watch out for self-seeded perennials on spring weeding forays

---

such as honesty, are rather coarse-leaved and can easily be mistaken for interlopers. Give plants a chance to reveal their identity: you will soon come to recognize the villains.

The foliage of established summer-flowering perennials will be burgeoning, providing a lovely setting for later spring bulbs such as tulips and daffodils planted in the border, or becoming a focal point in its own right: verbascums, for example,

produce steadily rising towers of whorled foliage that draw the eye for weeks before the first flowers open.

Some early spring-flowerers will by now be assuming the role of low foliage plants, ideal for groundcover. Other plants, such as some buttercups, will continue to bloom from spring well into summer. Some flower in succession for even longer (*see below*); in small gardens and restricted spaces, these are among the most valuable perennials, providing a display that begins in spring and continues through the season as neighboring plants change and develop.

PERSISTENT FLOWERERS

Perennial genera that start to bloom in spring and continue to produce flowers variably throughout the season include:

Aquilegia	*Filipendula*
Centranthus	*Geum*
Dianthus	*Malva*
Diascia	*Mimulus*
Dicentra	*Polemonium*
Epilobium	*Sidalcea*
Geranium	*Symphytum*

Deadheading and removing stems of spent flowers (*see p.56*) can also encourage many plants to prolong their flowering display.

PERENNIALS FOR SUMMER

A S SPRING GIVES WAY TO SUMMER, rising temperatures will encourage a surge of growth and, above all, a profusion of flowers. The number of summer-flowering perennials available is vast, but where space is at a premium it makes sense to choose varieties that, as individuals, provide both flowering and foliage interest and, collectively, a continuous succession of color.

HEAT AND LIGHT

Intense color is a feature of many summer-flowering perennials, whether it be the short-lived, blowsy beauty of rich pink and red Oriental poppies and peonies or the longer-lasting, shimmering blue haze of salvias and nepetas. As the season progresses, warm colors can easily dominate, as orange- and yellow-flowered daylilies (*Hemerocallis*) compete with red-hot pokers (*Kniphofia*) and crocosmias. Whether you find a general fiery effect stimulating or stifling is entirely a matter of personal taste. You can play it up, adding plants with bronze or purple foliage, or temper it by including pastel shades, such as pink-flowered *Geranium* x *oxonianum* 'Wargrave Pink', or a contrasting selection of blue or white flowers – the blue-tinged white flowers of *Campanula persicifolia* 'Chettle Charm' are ideal – and the occasional dash of steely or silvery foliage.

To get the best from summer perennials, site them where their flowers and foliage can be seen to their best advantage. Plants with deep colors, especially brilliant reds

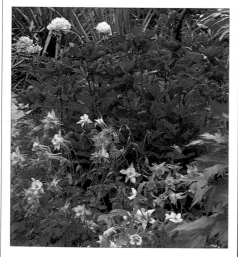

▲ A CLOSER LOOK
Summer provides a range of lovely flower forms to compare and contrast: here, bold peonies and clusters of delicate columbines.

► TURNING UP THE HEAT
The bronze-leaved dahlia 'Bishop of Llandaff' provides a stunning backdrop to yellow flowers and foliage.

▲ FRESH AS A DAISY
*Rudbeckias give a spectacular
show of flowers throughout
late summer and autumn. If
possible, plant in bold drifts.*

◄ LIGHT RELIEF
*Break up rich drifts of blue
(here from lavender and
campanulas) with fresh green
ferns and steely eryngiums.*

and oranges, often look best when given a prominent spot in the sun, whereas strong sunlight can bleach out pale colors. White and pastel shades light up shadier positions, and whites and blues become almost luminous as dusk deepens: these are the colors to plant on and around patios or wherever you like to sit on summer evenings. These are also spots where some priority to heat- and drought-tolerant perennials. Planting trees and shrubs to provide some shade will help less resilient plants ward off the effects of strong sun, but remember to adjust your choice of plants accordingly: too much shade will reduce the number and quality of the flowers of many sun-loving plants.

Scented plants in pale, luminous colors enhance evenings on the patio

fragrant plants, such as dictamnus and oenothera, are a must, whether you are entertaining in your summer garden or simply relaxing after a hot day's work.

Borders in exposed sites, on very free-draining sandy soils, are most likely to dry out in summer, so here it pays to give

PLANTS FOR DRY PLACES

You can improve the moisture-retentiveness of light, dry soil (*see pp.51, 54*), but good plant choice is also essential. Plants that will still put on a good show in hot, drought conditions include many with tuberous or thick roots, such as echinops, poppies, irises, and sisyrinchiums, together with those with succulent leaves and stems (such as sedums) or gray, downy, or hairy leaves: anthemis, artemisia, nepeta, osteospermum, phlomis, and stachys. Grasses, with a small leaf surface area that minimizes water loss, also stand up well.

PERENNIALS FOR AUTUMN

FAR FROM BEING A SEASON OF DECLINE, autumn can provide a curtain call for all the colors of summer. Indeed, many of the late-summer border perennials break through seasonal boundaries to give a succession of valuable flower and foliage interest until the first touch of frost. Foliage, grasses, and seedheads also play their part in broadening the autumn colorscape, with the leaves of many perennials changing color as temperatures drop.

THE DAISY FAMILY

Perennials with daisy-shaped flowers, such as asters, echinaceas, heleniums, and rudbeckias, many of North American origin, are great standbys for late summer and autumn. Perennial asters in particular make a superb show in shades of blue, lilac, cerise, pink, and white. All types of *Aster × frikartii*, such as lavender-blue 'Mönch', may well be in flower from midsummer until at least midautumn; in mild areas, even later. Other asters, such as semidouble, rich pink *Aster novi-angliae* 'Barr's Pink', provide a taller-growing and equally prolific show for weeks in late summer and early autumn.

PLANTING FOR COLOR

Sunflowers (*Helianthus*), bronze or yellow heleniums, yellow rudbeckias, and orange-centered pink echinaceas keep the warmth

▲ AUTUMN FAVORITES
Asters, especially mauve ones, are also known as Michaelmas daisies, after the traditional midautumn saint's day of the same name.

▼ LATE SHOW
Fantastic flower displays are possible in autumn: ribbons of pink asters are punctuated here by black-centered golden rudbeckias and the arching yellow plumes of goldenrod.

▲ LANDING PADS
*The flat flowerheads
of sedums are a late
treat for bees and
butterflies.*

◄ THINK PINK
*Clump-forming
Japanese anemones
will spread to form
drifts of fresh, pink
and white flowers.*

of summer in mind as autumn closes in. Goldenrod *(Solidago)* is another cheerful plant that spans the seasons, and the taller varieties make a fine yellow flower foil for blue asters. Most goldenrods, however, tend to be rampant colonizers, so choose carefully unless you are trying to fill a large area of wild garden. Golden yellow

---

The leaves of many perennials change color as temperatures drop

---

S. 'Laurin' is one of the best for smaller borders, since it does not grow to more than 24–30in/60–75cm tall, with an initial spread of around 18in/45cm.

In shady areas the beautiful pink or white chalices of Japanese anemones look superb, and the autumn display would be incomplete without at least one or two hardy chrysanthemums. Nor should some of the less well-known perennials be

overlooked. Bugbane *(Cimicifuga simplex)*, for instance, adds a graceful touch with its arching wands of small white flowers.

When autumn gives way to a mild winter, growth can continue, and it can be hard to decide when perennials have "finished" and should be cut down. There are no strict rules: as long as you are still enjoying a plant's appearance, you can delay cleaning it up, even until spring.

AS WINTER APPROACHES

Autumn is a time for clearing the garden by cutting plants back for the dormant season, but the stems and (particularly) seedheads of some perennials are worth keeping over winter for interest *(see next page)*. Consider leaving in place until spring:

Achillea	*Hakonechloa*
Astilbe	*Lunaria*
Carex	*Miscanthus*
Cortaderia	*Phlomis*
Echinops	*Sedum*
Eryngium	*Stipa*

PROLONGING THE SEASON

As WINTER APPROACHES, YOU COULD be forgiven for thinking that borders can present only a rather bleak picture. Yet cold weather often turns an otherwise boring outlook into a superb panorama, with snow coating every available surface and the low sun silhouetting the shapes of "freeze-dried" stems and seedheads. The absence of herbaceous perennials in flower during the colder months can be offset by the use of evergreens.

LATE WINTER INTEREST

Give those perennials that are in flower, such as hellebores and the beautiful winter-flowering *Iris unguicularis*, foils of solid foliage color: dark evergreen shrubs (both coniferous and broadleaved), for example, or bergenias, particularly those whose green summer leaves turn red with cold. Evergreens not only relieve the bareness of borders in winter, but they also give protection from cold and frost heaving to the crowns and roots below ground. Don't forget "ever-gray" perennials, too: the

SHOWN OFF AT THEIR BEST
Give those perennials in flower in late winter, such as these Helleborus foetidus, *a strong background – here the young red stems of a dogwood. Against a variegated shrub, their subtle flower color would be lost.*

foliage of *Stachys byzantina* will sparkle when frost gathers on its plush, feltlike leaf surfaces.

Perennials with warm foliage color are very welcome. The colors of some grasses, such as yellow-striped *Carex oshimensis*

> Evergreen groundcovers can relieve the bareness of borders in winter

'Evergold' and red-tinged *Hakonechloa macra* 'Aureola', persist, while others dry and fade to buff shades. Their stark forms, together with seedheads of plants such as eryngiums, phlomis, and sedums, are among the most beautiful sights in the winter garden when dusted with snow.

△ SHELTERED SCENE
The delicate-looking but surprisingly tough plumes and spikelets of grasses may persist through autumn and winter, dried to warm browns and beiges: if they are given some shelter, as here by shrubs, their stems will suffer less from battering by winter winds.

◁ FROSTED FORMS
Phlomis, asters, fennel, and, to the rear, a clump of miscanthus are among the plants left uncleared in this border, creating a perfectly preserved winter landscape glistening with frost.

PERENNIALS FOR COLOR

COLOR WHEEL

DO NOT BE AFRAID to experiment with color – the possibilities are endless. Choose combinations that appeal to you, rather than something you think you ought to like. Use the principles of the color wheel (*left*) to explore the way in which colors are related and why different types of color combination can create such different effects.

THE COLOR WHEEL

The wheel in its simplest form consists of three primary colors: red, blue, and yellow, which, when blended together, produce the secondary colors between them: purple, green, and orange. Infinite gradations of shade and hue occur where the segments meet. Colors farthest apart on the wheel contrast the most. The principal opposites occur between primary and secondary colors; purple and yellow, red and green, and blue and orange. Such combinations can produce bold and dazzling effects and are especially impressive when viewed from a distance. Some plants create their own vivid contrasts: the bright green leaf-fans and brilliant scarlet flowers of the crocosmia 'Lucifer', for example – but plant associations can be equally intense. Grouping blue-purple *Salvia × sylvestris*

COLOR CONTRASTS
Grouping together dissimilar, or directly contrasting, flower colors can be visually exciting. The violet campanula, for example, makes the yellow hemerocallis appear dazzlingly bright, while the purple-blue of the Ajuga reptans, *seen with the tangerine-colored geum, appears intense and vibrant. White, on the other hand, is perceived as reflected light in its purest form.*

MECONOPSIS BETONICIFOLIA

TROLLIUS × CULTORUM 'ALABASTER'

LEUCANTHEMUM × SUPERBUM

PAPAVER ORIENTALE 'MRS. PERRY'

ASTER AMELLUS 'NOCTURNE'

'May Night' with yellow *Oenothera*, for example, will excite the eye and accentuate the individual richness of their colors.

Using neighboring colors – pink *Papaver orientale* 'Mrs. Perry' with purple nepeta, perhaps – creates soft, harmonious combinations. From a distance the effect

In a red-themed border, will you include orange or crimson – or both?

may be a little hazy, but close up it will be subtle and elegant. Warm groupings of reds, orange, and gold (*see overleaf*) come to meet the eye, while cool purples and blues (*see pp.24–25*) create an illusion of distance. Planned color-themed plantings can be spectacular, expecially if you manage to maintain a continuity of color throughout the season. Remember, when planning on paper, that varying heights are particularly important when few colors are used. When listing plants to look for and buy, note their heights, too, so that any substitutions you choose or have to make will maintain the form as well as the color theme of your design.

FOLIAGE COLOR

Unusual leaf color plays a part in the most intriguing combinations: gold, lime, blue-gray, silver, copper, and purple. The way we perceive color is also affected by texture and light: yellow-splashed foliage, or fine silver or golden grasses, for example, give the illusion of dappled sunlight and lift colors around them.

CROCOSMIA 'LUCIFER'

GEUM RIVALE 'TANGERINE'

CAMPANULA CARPATICA

EUPHORBIA SCHILLINGII

AJUGA REPTANS 'ATROPURPUREA'

HEMEROCALLIS 'CONDILLA'

USING HOT COLORS

EVEN IN THE COOLEST OF SUMMERS, an illusion of warmth can be produced from plantings incorporating a liberal sprinkling of bright yellow, orange, and red flowers. There are relatively few fiery shades available for spring display, but colors intensify quite noticeably during summer months, with warm gold and russet tones becoming increasingly prominent with the onset of autumn.

A GLOWING YEAR

Doronicums and primroses are among the first perennials to make a sunny splash in spring, but it is the summer that ushers in the most dazzling hues. One of the first is *Geum* 'Borisii', which produces orange-scarlet flowers in early summer, sometimes with a later flush of coppery-hued blooms. Other easy choices include orange and red Oriental poppies, red peonies, crocosmias in fiery red, orange, and gold, and daylilies *(Hemerocallis)* in a huge range of of yellow, orange, rust, and red. Shortening days

BRINGING THE COLORS FORWARD
The free-flowering crocosmia 'Emily McKenzie' makes a lasting display, especially effective when set against yellow or purple.

encourage sedums, whose flat, rich rose-pink flowerheads are borne in profusion from late summer to autumn, together with heleniums, in yellow or the bronze-red of 'Moerheim Beauty'. Yellow rudbeckias may continue to flower until cut down by frost.

> Bronze or purple foliage intensifies hot flower colors

Warm color shades usually complement one another, so you can plant a selection of perennials to create distinct "hot spots." Orange and bright red shades also look particularly effective when set against a foil

▲ POWERFUL COMBINATION
The warmth of the orange daylilies exaggerates the cool purple of the agapanthus, making the daylilies appear closer than they really are.

▶ CONTRASTING FLOWER SHAPES
A variety of flower shapes is provided by this vivid collection of rudbeckias, monardas, dahlias, and tall-growing kniphofias.

of coppery purple leaves: for example, the bold foliage of *Rheum palmatum*, though it is extremely large. In a small space try clump-forming *Heuchera micrantha* 'Palace Purple', with metallic, dark purple leaves.

Some plants even provide their own foliage foil, such as moisture-loving *Lobelia* 'Queen Victoria', with blazing red spikes over purple-red foliage, and *Lychnis* × *arkwrightii*, sporting vermilion flowers set against purple-bronze leaves.

RECOMMENDED

SPRING-FLOWERING
Doronicum 'Miss Mason'
Oenothera fruticosa 'Fyrverkeri'
Primula rosea

SUMMER-FLOWERING
Achillea filipendulina 'Gold Plate'
Crocosmia × *crocosmiiflora* 'Emily McKenzie'
Hemerocallis fulva 'Flore Pleno'
Kniphofia triangularis

Lychnis chalcedonica
Monarda 'Cambridge Scarlet'
Paeonia officinalis 'Rubra Plena'
Papaver orientale 'Allegro'

AUTUMN-FLOWERING
Helenium 'Butterpat'
Lobelia 'Queen Victoria'
Rudbeckia 'Herbstsonne'
Sedum 'Ruby Glow'

USING COOL COLORS

THE FRESHNESS OF SPRING can be enhanced and midsummer heat relieved in part by planting perennials in cool shades. Blue and white schemes are the obvious choices but can be stark; a sprinkling of restrained hues such as pale yellow, greens, and soft pinks enhance the effect. Cool shades can also be combined with contrasting colors to produce deliberate clashes of color.

KEEPING IT COOL

Cool schemes are easy to carry through the spring and most of the summer, starting with white and pink-flushed hellebores, perhaps supplemented by wood anemones, white and blue varieties of *Primula denticulata*, soft pink or white bergenias, and the Siberian forget-me-not *(Brunnera)*. These are followed by pink, blue, or white campanulas; blue or white monkshoods *(Aconitum)*; hardy geraniums in every shade of blue, purple, pink, and white; and catmint, *Nepeta × faassenii*, which produces aromatic, gray-

> Cool color schemes can
> be enhanced with silver
> or white foliage plants

green leaves topped by soft lavender-blue flowers. Colors tend to heat up in late summer, but it is possible for beds and borders to keep their cool with plenty of foliage and elegant, white-flowered Japanese anemones.

HEIGHT OF ELEGANCE
Flower spires in cool shades give a fresh, airy look. The odd warmer hue, here from the verbascum 'Helen Johnson', will not intrude among (from left) *delphiniums, campanulas, and dicentras.*

BORDER HIGHLIGHTS
*Lime green flatters hot colors but also adds
freshness to cool schemes: here, euphorbia and
alchemilla are set against a dark background.*

ALSO RECOMMENDED

SPRING-FLOWERING
Aconitum 'Bressingham Spire'
Anemone nemerosa (wood anemone)
Bergenia 'Silberlicht'; *Helleborus foetidus*
Primula denticulata var. *alba*
Pulmonaria saccharata 'Argentea'

SUMMER-FLOWERING
Alchemilla mollis; *Campanula* 'Burghaltii'
Geranium pratense 'Mrs. Kendall Clark'
Leucanthemum × *superbum* 'Esther Read'

AUTUMN-FLOWERING
Anemone × *hybrida* 'Honorine Jobert'
Cimicifuga simplex 'Elstead'
Eryngium oliverianum
Ergyngium variifolium

HIGHLIGHTING THE EFFECT

An almost snowy scene can be achieved by restricting your choice of plants to those producing white flowers; alternatively, plant only blue-flowered subjects for an even chillier display. The cooling effect can be further emphasized by adding silver- or gray-leaved foliage plants, several of which conveniently produce flowers in complementary shades. The prickly-leaved sea hollies (*Eryngium*) with white or silver foliage and blue and silver flowerheads are good examples, as is felt-leaved *Stachys byzantina* 'Silver Carpet'. A nonflowering but evergreen plant, it can be used in white or blue planting schemes and makes an excellent mat of silver-gray groundcover.

COOL COMPANIONS
*This subtle blend of cool flower colors is
further enhanced by the aromatic bronze-
purple fennel foliage.*

PLANTING PLANS FOR PERENNIALS

CHOOSING PLANS AND STYLES

THE BEST RESULTS (and least work) are achieved by choosing designs that blend well with their surroundings and contain plants that are naturally suited to the conditions imposed by the site. A plant that needs moisture, for example, will never be happy in poor, fast-draining ground, and it will need frequent watering in a terracotta pot. The following pages contain planting ideas that will work equally well in urban or rural settings and have been designed for a range of environments, from sun to shade and poolside to trough.

TRADITIONAL BORDER STYLE

A well-planned herbaceous border can provide a breathtaking panorama of color from spring until the first frosts of autumn. Until quite recently, such borders were planned on a lavish scale, integrating bold drifts of flowers with bands of attractive foliage. Today, it is perfectly possible to adapt the style for smaller gardens, and using carefully chosen perennials that suit your site and soil will cut down the time needed for maintenance. You will need to include plants of varying heights; to minimize the need for staking, choose compact, self-supporting varieties of tall plants where available. Plants with interesting foliage will contribute to the display even when not in flower.

▶ TENDING YOUR BORDER
For a traditional look, plants are kept neat and are not allowed to flop. Twiggy sticks (right) *make unobtrusive supports and will not spoil the look of the border. Regularly removing dead flowerheads* (far right) *helps encourage further flowering on many plants and keeps the border looking neat.*

PROVIDING SUPPORT P.55   PROLONGING FLOWERING P.56

◀ POSITIONING PLANTS *Well-spaced plants limit the areas in which weeds can appear.*

A Traditional Herbaceous Border

This long, narrow border in sun contains fairly easygoing plants for an average soil, its texture improved by good preparation (*see p.50*). Yellow doronicums and pink bergenias make an early display; they have finished flowering in this illustration (*continued on pp.30–31*). Campanulas, lychnis, and anthemis follow on closely behind, then the flamboyant crocosmias which, with asters and helianthus, keep the show going in late summer.

PLANTING PLAN

1 3 *Anthemis punctata* subsp. *cupaniana*, 14in/35cm apart
2 3 *Aster novi-belgii* 'Little Pink Beauty', 18in/45cm apart
3 4 *Lychnis chalcedonica*, 14in/35cm apart
4 2 *Campanula glomerata* 'Purple Pixie', 12in/30cm apart
5 1 *Helianthus* 'Loddon Gold'
6 3 *Bergenia* 'Baby Doll', 12in/30cm apart
7 3 *Crocosmia* 'Lucifer', 14in/35cm apart

8 2 *Doronicum* 'Miss Mason', 18in/45cm apart
9 2 *Aster* × *frikartii* 'Mönch', 16in/40cm apart

6½ft/2m

20ft/6m

Aster novi-belgii 'Little Pink Beauty' will produce better flowers if you thin some shoots in spring (*see p.56*).

Anthemis punctata subsp. *cupaniana* produces its daisy flowers throughout summer if given a sunny site. The silvery leaves are also decorative.

Lychnis chalcedonica is an erect plant that needs no staking. In summer it produces heads of star-shaped, scarlet flowers.

Bergenia 'Baby Doll' has pink flowers in early and midspring that gradually darken with age.

Helianthus 'Loddon Gold' is a perennial sunflower that adds height to the border.

Crocosmia 'Lucifer', with its strong arching stems, is one of the easiest crocosmias to grow.

CAMPANULA GLOMERATA *'Purple Pixie' starts to flower in early summer. Deadheading prolongs its season.*

ASTER × FRIKARTII *'Mönch' is an excellent cultivar of this long-flowering and disease-resistant garden stalwart.*

Doronicum 'Miss Mason' bears bright yellow daisy flowers in mid- and late spring, held high above the foliage.

TRADITIONAL BORDER *continued*

Verbascum chaixii 'Gainsborough' bears stately spikes of light yellow flowers over woolly foliage.

Achillea filipendulina 'Gold Plate' forms evergreen clumps of gray-green leaves. A few flowerheads, produced all summer, could be sacrificed for dried arrangements.

Helenium 'Coppelia' has copper-orange flowers that give the border a warm glow from midsummer to early autumn.

DIANTHUS 'MRS. SINKINS'
A well-known, deliciously scented, old-fashioned pink. When plants become scruffy, renew them by layering (see p.61).

PLANTING PLAN

10 3 *Helenium* 'Coppelia',
     18in/45cm apart
11 3 *Dianthus* 'Mrs Sinkins',
     12in/30cm apart
12 2 *Verbascum chaixii*
     'Gainsborough',
     18in/45cm apart

13 2 *Sedum* 'Ruby Glow',
     14in/35cm apart
14 2 *Echinops bannaticus*,
     3ft/90cm apart
15 3 *Achillea filipendulina*
     'Gold Plate', 2ft/60cm apart
16 2 *Salvia* × *superba*,
     18in/45cm apart

6½ft/2m

20ft/6m

MORE CHOICES

Other relatively easygoing
perennials well suited to the
formally kept style are:

CLUMP-FORMING
Alstroemeria Ligtu Hybrids
Aquilegia McKana Group
Echinacea purpurea 'Robert
    Bloom'
Hemerocallis 'Green Flutter'
Heuchera 'Pewter Moon'
Gypsophila paniculata
    'Bristol Fairy'
Monarda 'Croftway Pink'
Nepeta 'Six Hills Giant'
Paeonia lactiflora 'Bowl of
    Beauty'
Papaver orientale
    'Perry's White'
Phlox paniculata 'Prince of
    Orange'
Physostegia virginiana
Scabiosa caucasica 'Clive
    Greaves'
Sidalcea 'Elsie Heugh'
Stokesia laevis 'Blue Star'
Thalictrum delavayi
    'Hewitt's Double'

SPIKES AND SPIRES
Delphinium 'Blue Nile'
Iris 'Vanity'
Kniphofia 'Royal Standard'
Liatris spicata 'Kobold'
Lupinus 'The Chatelaine'
Schizostylis coccinea
    'Major'
Veronica 'Shirley Blue'

FOLIAGE INTEREST
Artemisia 'Powis Castle'
Eryngium bourgatii
Euphorbia griffithii
    'Dixter'
Phlomis russeliana
Stachys byzantina 'Silver
    Carpet'

*Additional details can be
found in* Recommended
Perennials, *pp.64–77.*

ECHINOPS BANNATICUS
*The hairy, gray-green leaves
surround woolly stems topped
by bluish gray flowers that
will attract butterflies and
bees to the border from mid-
to late summer.*

Salvia × *superba* has spikes of
purple flowers that contrast in
shape and color with the
neighboring achillea.

Sedum 'Ruby Glow' softens the border's edge
with its fleshy, purple-green leaves and soft
red flowers at the end of summer.

NATURALISTIC PLANTING

Traditionally neat borders appeal to orderly minded gardeners, but perennials also lend themselves to a wilder, more informal style. Almost any perennial can be used in this way, but careful grouping is needed to achieve even the most artless-seeming effect. The plan on the next page has been designed to create a manageable border; repeating some of the plants elsewhere in the garden creates the impression that they have spread naturally.

CREATING AN INFORMAL EFFECT

Don't be cautious; use bold perennials, such as rudbeckias and goldenrod in asymmetrical drifts, with low-growing, self-seeding plants such as alchemillas as dense groundcover to suppress weeds around taller plants. These will need to be robust to resist being swamped by the spreading plants. Wild species are often bigger than named varieties, with a greater proportion of foliage to flowers: this can also look more natural than highly bred, floriferous plants in unexpected flower colors.

PERENNIALS IN GRASS

The meadow look is much coveted, but establishing perennials in grass is not easy. For a much more manageable planting, simply include some ornamental grasses (*see box on the next page*) among other perennials. Plant them in groups to create natural-looking ribbons and drifts of grass surrounding the flowering plants. These grasses and other plants will compete on equal terms for the nutrients and moisture in the soil, and identifying and removing perennial weeds will be much easier.

▶ NATURAL COLONIZERS *Opportunist self-seeders such as columbines soon fill gaps between purchased plants, heightening the informal effect in which plants are allowed to spread, reducing the space available for weeds.*

◀ PROVIDING GREENERY *Plume poppies (here with campanulas) are valuable for foliage interest.*

PLAN FOR AN INFORMAL BORDER

This plan, shown in summer, includes easy-to-grow perennials tolerant of a variety of soils and a degree of summer neglect. Apart from two irresistible cultivars of geranium and plume poppy (*Macleaya*), it consists of more naturalistic-looking species plants. Foliage interest is supplied by architectural plants such as acanthus and plume poppy, while the inclusion of grasses echoes the latest garden design trends.

PLANTING PLAN

1 1 *Acanthus mollis*
2 3 *Geranium pratense* 'Plenum Caeruleum', 2ft/60cm apart
3 3 *Rudbeckia laciniata*, 2ft/60cm apart
4 3 *Athyrium filix-femina*, 20in/50cm apart
5 2 *Macleaya microcarpa* 'Kelway's Coral Plume', 3ft/90cm apart
6 1 *Carex pendula*
7 5 *Leucanthemum vulgare*, 12in/30cm apart
8 2 *Campanula latiloba*, 18in/45cm apart
9 3 *Aquilegia vulgaris*, 12in/30cm apart
10 2 *Briza media*, 20in/50cm apart

4½ft/1.5m

9ft/3m

Acanthus mollis has handsome leaves and flowers that develop into polished seeds of rich russet.

Rudbeckia laciniata has deeply cut leaves and yellow flowers with central cones of greenish yellow.

GERANIUM PRATENSE 'Plenum Caeruleum' is a double-flowered version of the geranium that grows wild in meadows. Its foliage colors well in autumn.

Athyrium filix-femina, the lady fern, forms a delicate mass of green fronds.

USING ORNAMENTAL GRASSES

Most ornamental grasses are unfussy and can be treated just like other perennials, cutting them back in spring to remove messy growth, being careful not to damage emerging leaf tips. There are silvery and gold-leaved grasses and even some with banded foliage that give the illusion of dappled sunlight. Their waving movement gives a lovely, naturalistic effect. More and more small, clump-forming grasses are becoming widely available. Miscanthus (*right*) and cortaderia can form very large clumps: a row of these as a backdrop to an informal border is useful for reducing wind in an exposed site. *For more details, see p.71.*

M. SINENSIS 'ZEBRINUS'

Macleaya microcarpa 'Kelway's Coral Plume' adds hazy height to the planting with its clouds of tiny flowers.

Leucanthemum vulgare bears simple daisy flowers in late spring and early summer.

Carex pendula, a tufted, evergreen sedge, gives year-round interest, especially if the drooping seedheads are left on the plant.

Campanula latiloba makes evergreen basal rosettes of foliage from which shoot spires of blue bells in summer.

Briza media, the quaking grass, adds texture both with its foliage and its oatlike seedheads.

...gia vulgaris, or ...bine, will scatter ...ds with abandon.

PLANTING IN SHADE

Some shade is always an asset in the garden, and there are many perennials that will not only tolerate but positively thrive in a site sheltered from all-day sun. The degree of shade, however, will affect what you can grow; as the depth and period of shade increase, so the choice of plants decreases. The planting plan on the next page shows a range of flowering and foliage plants that will all thrive in shade and lists some alternatives.

DEALING WITH SHADE IN THE GARDEN

The density of shade can vary greatly. Under deciduous trees, you can make the most of the light early in the year to grow colorful bulbs among other spring-flowering plants. In dappled shade, where trees and shrubs are not densely planted, or in areas that the sun reaches for only part of the day, cyclamen, violas, and primroses can provide spring interest, and summer perennials such as astilbes and aruncus will flower well. Generally, only foliage plants can cope with the day-long, year-round shade cast by evergreens or tall buildings. Here, ferns and hostas come into their own and combine well with bronze-leaved bergenias and spotted pulmonarias.

PRACTICAL TIPS

• Trees and shrubs overshadowing perennials will also compete with them for food and water. Water young perennials regularly until they are established, and mulch areas in the rain shadow in spring while the ground is wet. Plants may also benefit from a balanced fertilizer. This must not be applied, however, when soil is dry, or it may damage plants.

• A wall or tree that casts shade is also likely to create a rain shadow. Check that plants have sufficient water during dry spells.

• Plants in the shadow of a dull, dark wall will immediately look brighter and livelier if the wall is painted white. The wall will reflect light into the area, cheering it up and also benefiting the plants.

SPRING PLANTS UNDER A DECIDUOUS TREE
Naturalized bulbs flower beneath a deciduous tree before it has come into leaf; their leaves will die back into the wild grass for summer.

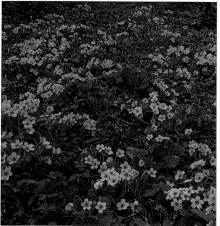

SPRING PLANTS IN LIGHT SHADE
Early-flowering primroses and violas will carpet the ground around shrubs and will appreciate their shade later in the summer.

⋘ GREEN PARTNERS *Blue-green hostas and ferns are great standbys for shade.*

PLAN FOR A SHADY CORNER

This planting capitalizes on the fact that shaded soil often holds moisture well, but drier soil can be mulched (*see p.54*). The chalice flowers of hellebores are sometimes in full display by mid-January, quickly followed by the clustered blooms of bergenias. Pink, blue, and white are the dominant summer flower colors, with more interest introduced by a yellow foxglove, the textured hostas, and purple-green fern fronds of athyrium.

Polygonatum falcatum 'Variegatum', a stripe-leaved Solomon's seal, adds an elegant arching shape to the planting.

Polystichum setiferum is a tall, evergreen fern, useful for providing color and architectural interest during winter.

HELLEBORUS ORIENTALIS
Cup-shaped flowers, sometimes spotted, open from midwinter to early spring. Cut away old, tattered foliage, which detracts from their beauty.

Omphalodes verna has bright blue flowers that can be damaged by a late frost.

BERGENIA 'SILBERLICHT'
A vigorous cultivar with leathery, evergreen leaves and white flowers in spring that age gracefully to pink.

Brunnera macrophylla has forget-me-not-like flowers in spring. It self-seeds prolifically.

Athyrium niponicum var. *pictum* has fronds suffused with purple, green, and silver-gray.

Hosta sieboldiana has huge leaves and later produces pale lilac flowers.

PLANTING PLAN

7ft/2.2m

8ft/2.5m

1 2 *Omphalodes verna*, 18in/45cm apart
2 1 *Bergenia* 'Silberlicht'
3 3 *Digitalis grandiflora*, 12in/30cm apart
4 3 *Polygonatum falcatum* 'Variegatum', 12in/30cm apart
5 1 *Helleborus orientalis*
6 2 *Brunnera macrophylla*, 18in/45cm apart
7 3 *Polystichum setiferum*, 12in/30cm apart
8 2 *Athyrium niponicum* var. *pictum*, 18in/45cm apart
9 1 *Hosta sieboldiana*
10 4 *Tiarella wherryi*, 10in/25cm apart
11 1 *Dicentra spectabilis*
12 2 *Campanula latifolia*, 2ft/60cm apart

Campanula latifolia produces deep violet or white bell flowers in summer.

DIGITALIS GRANDIFLORA
This unusual foxglove has pale yellow flowers in early to midsummer above clumps of evergreen leaves.

Dicentra spectabilis produces its locket flowers in late spring and early summer.

Tiarella wherryi has clouds of small, pinkish flowers in late spring and early summer.

MORE CHOICES

FOR DRY SHADE
Carex pendula
Iris foetidissima
Lunaria rediviva
Paeonia emodi

FOR MOIST SHADE
Kirengeshoma palmata
Matteuccia struthiopteris
Osmunda regalis

AS GROUNDCOVER
Anemone × *hybrida*
Pulmonaria
Polypodium vulgare (fern)

PLANTING IN MOIST GROUND

Plants that need free-draining soil will not only fail to thrive but often rot in damp ground, but there are plenty of attractive perennials that relish a constant supply of moisture at their roots. Many tolerate seasonal flooding, but, unlike true aquatic species, most dislike having wet feet all the time. If you love these plants yet do not have a suitable spot for them, a plastic-lined bog garden (*below*) is not only easy to make but very water-efficient.

CONSTRUCTING A BOG GARDEN

The edges of informal pools (*see next page*) are prime sites for bog plants, but it is also easy and inexpensive to create your own bog garden. Excavate a bowl-shaped hole at least 18in/45cm deep. Rake the area, remove any sharp stones, and line with thick plastic sheeting. Pierce the base of the liner in plenty of places with a garden fork to prevent excess waterlogging, and cover with a 2in/5cm layer of very coarse sand. Fill up with a soil mix (*see below*), then water thoroughly before planting.

PRACTICAL TIPS

• If the surface of the soil seems dry, it's time to water again.
• A thick mulch of bark chips over the soil helps slow down evaporation.
• To make it easy to restore water levels, bury a seep or perforated hose in the sand layer, with the underground end blocked.
• In a larger bog garden, stepping stones or log sections allow easy access and will prevent the moist soil from becoming compacted as you work around the plants.

PLANTS FOR A DAMP ENVIRONMENT
There are many ordinary perennials and, especially, ferns that will enjoy these moist conditions, but for a wider choice try looking also in the water plant section of nurseries for semi-aquatics such as marsh marigolds (Caltha palustris).

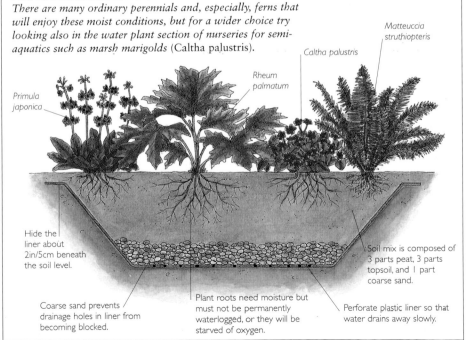

Matteuccia
struthiopteris

Caltha palustris

Rheum
palmatum

Primula
japonica

Hide the liner about 2in/5cm beneath the soil level.

Soil mix is composed of 3 parts peat, 3 parts topsoil, and 1 part coarse sand.

Coarse sand prevents drainage holes in liner from becoming blocked.

Plant roots need moisture but must not be permanently waterlogged, or they will be starved of oxygen.

Perforate plastic liner so that water drains away slowly.

◄LUXURIANT SCENE *Lush green hostas provide a vibrant foil for pink persicarias.*

PLAN FOR A WATERSIDE PLANTING

This plan is ideal for any modest area of moist soil – for example, beside a garden pool, as here, where the reflection of the plants in the water will enhance the effect considerably. It has been designed to provide a display of colorful flowers from spring until late summer (it is shown here in early summer). The scarlet mimulus in particular is invaluable for its long flowering season, while the variegated hosta adds foliage interest.

PLANTING PLAN

1 3 *Mimulus cupreus* 'Whitecroft Scarlet', 12in/30cm apart
2 3 *Iris sibirica*, 18in/45cm apart
3 2 *Persicaria bistorta* 'Superba', 2ft/60cm apart
4 1 *Hosta* 'Shade Fanfare'
5 1 *Trollius europaeus*
6 3 *Primula japonica*, 14in/35cm apart

Mimulus cupreus 'Whitecroft Scarlet' is rather short-lived but produces a brilliant show of flowers as it spreads along the water's edge.

PRIMULA JAPONICA
One of the candelabra primroses, which make charming poolside plants. Divide congested clumps in late summer when leaves are dying down.

IRIS SIBIRICA
The violet flowers stand up well above the clumps of strap-shaped leaves in summer. There are many types of Siberian iris in different colors to choose from; shades available include good blues, light yellow, deeper purples, dark red, and white.

PLANT CHOICES

Many plants grown on damp ground tend to become very large, so choose carefully if space is limited. Rheums, ligularias, gunneras, *Iris laevigata,* and *Rodgersia pinnata* are often grown by poolsides, yet all are very vigorous and will dominate small sites. If you want a lush, leafy look but do not have much space, focus on interesting foliage and warm, vivid flower tones: a variety of ferns, perhaps, interspersed with the rich purple leaves and scarlet flower spikes of the perennial lobelias 'Queen Victoria' or 'Dark Crusader', or the mahogany stems and coppery pink flowers of the geum 'Leonard's Variety'.

Persicaria bistorta 'Superba' flowers over a long period. It can be invasive, but unwanted patches are easily uprooted.

Hosta 'Shade Fanfare' produces a bonus of short spires of lavender-blue, funnel-shaped flowers in summer.

Trollius europaeus produces lemon yellow, double buttercup-like flowers in early and midsummer.

PERENNIALS IN CONTAINERS

Many perennials will grow happily in containers. For practical reasons, small and medium-sized plants are usually best, though where a dramatic effect is required, tall plants such as phormiums make excellent focal points. Low, trailing plants can be used to soften pot or tub edges. Remember that foliage color, texture, and shape is highlighted in raised plantings. Evergreens are invaluable, giving pleasure through the year.

CHOOSING THE RIGHT CONTAINER

The choice of container is enormous: glazed bowls and urns, terracotta or plastic pots, traditional half barrels, and stone sinks. Choose materials that tie in with other hard surfaces in your garden, such as brickwork. If plants are to be in containers for more than one season, they must have room for their roots; small containers also lose moisture too quickly. All plants in containers will need regular watering and occasional repotting. Choose frostproof materials that will be as hardy as the perennials you plant in them, or, if you wish to use more fragile containers for summer display, put plants in their own pots within them to minimize root disturbance.

PRACTICAL TIPS

• Before planting, soak new terracotta pots in water overnight to reduce water loss from the soil mix into the porous clay.
• A soil-based mix is best for long-term perennials. Use an acidic mix for lime-hating plants.
• Keep drainage holes free by raising containers off the ground on blocks or bricks, or use terracotta feet.
• Slow-release fertilizer granules keep plants well-fed for about a season, or apply liquid feed at intervals during the growing season.
• Unless you want to group plants with similar needs, such as rock plants, giving plants the right growing conditions is much easier if you use only one plant per container.

Fill two-thirds of the bucket with water

WATERING BEFORE PLANTING
Submerge the plant, still in its pot, in a bucket of water. The rootball is thoroughly soaked when bubbles stop appearing.

Plunge the pot in water

Make sure that the drainage holes at the base of the pot are not blocked

PROVIDING SOME DRAINAGE
Before adding soil mix, put a layer of material such as terracotta pieces in the base of a container, especially one without a drainage hole.

◄PINK AND GREEN *Pinks, as in these geranium flowers, look surprisingly good with terracotta.*

PLAN FOR A GROUP OF CONTAINERS

This grouping provides a long season of interest. Early violets and pulsatillas are followed by campanulas and diascias with creeping thyme. These shallow-rooting plants are happy in a trough.

Agapanthus provides a tall focal point; geraniums flower all season long, while heucheras give year-round foliage interest. These need deeper pots (here 20in/50cm deep and across at the rim).

PLANTING PLAN

1 1 *Geranium* × *oxonianum*
2 1 *Heuchera micrantha* 'Palace Purple'
3 1 *Thymus serpyllum*
4 1 *Viola riviniana* Purpurea Group
5 2 *Diascia* 'Salmon Supreme'
6 3 *Pulsatilla vulgaris*
7 1 *Campanula portenschlagiana*
8 2 *Geranium* × *cantabrigiense* 'Biokovo'
9 3 *Agapanthus campanulatus* 'Isis'

Geranium × *oxonianum* produces its dainty pink flowers from late spring until autumn.

Heuchera micrantha 'Palace Purple' bears airy cream flowers followed by rose pink seedheads.

Thymus serpyllum will creep over the sides of a trough. It has whorls of purple flowers in summer.

VIOLA RIVINIANA
Purplish leaves set off these light violet flowers. It will readily self-seed into paving cracks around any container.

Diascia 'Salmon Supreme' will flower nonstop from summer to midautumn.

ALSO RECOMMENDED FOR CONTAINERS

FLOWERING PLANTS
Dicentra spectabilis 'Alba'
Limonium (statice), especially
   L. platyphyllum 'Violetta'
Osteospermum, especially
   'Stardust'
Primroses: *Primula allionii*,
   P. rosea; *P. vulgaris* subsp.
   sibthorpii; *P. denticulata*
Viola cornuta

FOLIAGE PLANTS
Carex flagellifera
Hosta 'Ginko Craig', 'Ground
   Master', 'Golden Tiara',
   H. ventricosa
Hakonechloa macra 'Aureola'
Houttuynia cordata
   'Chameleon'
Mentha suaveolens 'Variegata'
Sedum spathulifolium

CREEPING PLANTS
Arabis
Aubrieta
Campanula cochleariifolia
   'Flore Pleno'
Dryas octopetala
Sedum acre 'Aureum'
Sempervivum, especially
   S. arachnoideum subsp.
   tomentosum

Agapanthus campanulatus 'Isis'
grows to 30in/75cm and has
dark blue flowers in mid- to
late summer. If container-grown
it will require protection during
winter north of Zone 7.

Geranium x cantabrigiense
'Biokovo' is a compact plant
with pinkish white flowers in
summer.

PULSATILLA VULGARIS
These silky spring flowers are
followed by equally delightful
seedheads. It must have sun
and good drainage.

Campanula portenschlagiana is
good for softening the sides of a
trough. Flowers cover the plant in
midsummer, and the leaves are
evergreen. Keep it in check, or it
will swamp other plants.

LOOKING AFTER PERENNIALS

GIVING PLANTS A GOOD START

PLANTING AND CARING FOR YOUR perennials can be very rewarding, and the most valuable time you can spend on them is right at the start — choosing the right plants for your soil and site, preparing the ground well, selecting healthy specimens, and planting them with care are the key tasks that will repay themselves all through the season with a healthy, vigorous display.

SECRETS OF SUCCESSFUL GARDENING

Garden tasks need not be a burden and can even be enjoyable. They give you the chance to appreciate your plants at close quarters and the pleasure of seeing your choices reemerge, develop, flower, and fade during every season of the year.

"Little and often" is the secret to stop garden tasks from building up into a lot of work. If you find time regularly to take a stroll around your garden or patio inspecting your plants, you will be able to nip all sorts of problems in the bud immediately and help your plants look their best. Uprooting weeds as they emerge is not only easier than removing them when large, it also means less disturbance to your plants' roots.

Plant problems are best dealt with before they are able to take hold: simply picking off a pest or an affected shoot may be enough to stop the problem in its tracks. Regular deadheading improves and extends many plants' flowering display. Water your new plants well, and they shouldn't need it when mature – saving hours of work (and precious water). And if you find staking a chore, choose sturdy perennials that do not need support.

USEFUL PLANT TERMS

• **Crown** Base of a plant, where roots and stems join.
• **Cultivar** Variation on a natural *species* that is selected or bred for a special characteristic. The breeder chooses a name for the plant, for example *Dicentra* 'Stuart Boothman'.
• **Dormancy** Pause of plant growth and activity, usually during cold winter months.
• **Flowerhead** Mass of small flowers that appear to form a single flower.
• **Genus** Group of plant *species* that share a range of characteristics, such as *Dicentra*.
• **Hybrid** Cross-breed of different *species*, indicated by the symbol 'x' in the Latin name.
• **Rhizome** Underground, creeping, thick fleshy stem that sends out roots and shoots.
• **Root ball** Roots and surrounding soil visible when plant is removed from pot.
• **Species** Group of plants that can breed together to produce similar offspring, for example *Dicentra spectabilis*.
• **Subspecies, variety, form** Naturally occurring variations within a *species*, with an additional name in italics following the abbreviations subsp., var. and f. For example *Dicentra spectabilis* f. *alba*, a white-flowered form of the pink-flowered species.

◄ POPPY APPEAL *In early summer, Oriental poppies add a fresh touch to long-flowering euphorbias.*

PREPARING THE GROUND

B EFORE PLANTING PERENNIA'.S, it is essential to prepare the site thoroughly; once they begin to grow and spread, access to the soil will be much more difficult. If a site has been neglected, your first task will be to remove any perennial weeds. The soil should then be dug over or turned over – a rototiller is a boon where there are large areas of soil – and, unless your soil is very rich, organic materials added to improve soil structure and quality.

CLEARING WEEDS

On new ground that you want to prepare for planting, you must first remove any persistent perennial weeds, such as quack grass and bindweed, either with weedkiller or by conscientious hand-clearing, since their roots spread widely underground and will infest those of your plants. If the site is badly infested, it is well worth spraying the whole area with a systemic weedkiller the season before planting. Other weeds, such as crabgrass and dandelions, will lurk in the soil as seeds and spring up throughout the year; they can be hoed off as they appear. Even when you don't have time to hoe, pick off any weed flowerheads you see before they have the chance to set seed.

USING WEEDKILLER

• Always seek advice at your local garden center before buying and using weedkiller.
• "Contact" weedkiller destroys annual weeds but makes only the top growth of perennial weeds die down; the roots survive.
• "Systemic" weedkiller destroys foliage, stems, and roots of both annual and perennial weeds, without affecting the soil. It is most effective when weeds are in full growth.
• Use spray systemic weedkiller only where there are no garden plants.
• Whenever possible, apply spot treatment with a brush so as not to harm other plants.
• Some perennial weeds may need more than one treatment.

REMOVING WEEDS BY HAND
Fork up the weed, holding main stems close to the soil as you lift to help get as much of the root up as possible. Fork over and sift to remove stray pieces of root that will regrow.

USING BLACK PLASTIC
If you can delay planting for a season or two, cover the area with a sheet of thick black plastic to starve weeds of light. Anchor the edges in the soil using a spade.

MAKING DIGGING EASIER

Digging over a large area is much easier if you follow a methodical pattern. Single digging (*see below*) breaks up and aerates soil without bringing the lower, infertile subsoil to the surface. You can also take the opportunity to fork in organic matter in the base of the trenches. Do not dig when the soil is wet or you will damage the soil structure. Keep your back straight and take a break as soon as you feel tired.

FIRST TRENCH
Mark out small, manageable areas. Starting in one corner, dig out a trench one spit (spade blade) deep and about 12in/30cm wide. Reserve the soil you remove; this will be used to fill the last trench that you dig.

REMAINING AREA
Working backward so as not to compact the soil, dig a second trench, turning soil into the first. Bury any annual weeds. Continue until the area is dug, filling the last trench with the soil from the first.

USING A ROTOTILLER

If you are planning to use a rototiller for large, neglected areas, it is essential that you clear the garden of perennial weeds first. Otherwise, the blades will chop up their roots into tiny pieces, each with the potential to regrow, vastly multiplying the problem. When hiring or buying machinery, for safety's sake, ask for a demonstration first. Wear goggles and keep a firm grip as you work.

IMPROVING YOUR SOIL STRUCTURE

Digging and forking improve the soil structure to some extent, but it can be further improved by the addition of well-rotted organic matter. This will enhance the soil's drainage, aeration, fertility, and moisture-holding properties. Adding the material in the season prior to planting will give it time to become well incorporated.

ENRICHING YOUR SOIL
Fork in organic materials such as compost, well-rotted manure, composted bark, or leafmold. Repeat in subsequent years.

LEVELING THE SURFACE
Before planting, use a wide-tined rake to break up remaining clods of soil on the surface; this makes weeding much easier.

PLANTING PERENNIALS

MANY PERENNIALS ARE SOLD as container-grown plants, which can be planted at any time during the growing season. The traditional times to plant – spring and autumn – are the best, since mild, damp weather helps plants establish well. Avoid planting in hot, sunny weather because of the difficulty of keeping the plants watered sufficiently. Plants will also suffer a check to growth.

CHOOSING A HEALTHY PLANT

Do not buy perennials showing signs of disease or neglect, such as wilted leaves or a mass of roots appearing out of the bottom of the container. Look for plants with sturdy topgrowth and thick, strong stems. Do not buy a plant with tangled roots coming out of the base of its pot, or one growing among weeds and moss.

MONEY-SAVING TIP

Do not judge a plant by its size, since an older, bigger one may take a long time to get established. A smaller specimen with good fresh growth will be less expensive and grow quickly. Once established, it can be divided to produce more plants (see p.57).

Weak, spindly topgrowth

Moss and weeds growing on soil mix

Old, woody base

BADLY GROWN PLANT
This plant's poor topgrowth and signs of moss and weeds growing on the soil mix indicate lack of care and nourishment.

POTBOUND PLANT
Never buy plants with roots wound around the inside of the pot. Plants like this are almost impossible to establish successfully.

Potbound roots form a tight, congested mass

Strong, healthy topgrowth with unmarked leaves

Clean, moist soil mix

Established, vigorous roots

HEALTHY PLANT
This specimen is healthy and weed-free. Other excellent signs include short, stocky growth, lots of shoots, and well-developed roots.

PLANTING CONTAINER-GROWN PERENNIALS

Never plant in frozen or very dry soil – this usually ends in disaster. Before planting a group of plants, set them out in their pots to find the best arrangement and spacing. Water well before and after planting.

PRACTICAL TIP

To water purchased plants really thoroughly before planting, soak them in their pots in a bucket of water for about 15 minutes.

1 **Dig a planting hole** twice as wide and to the correct depth *(see below)*. Tap the pot to slide out the plant.

2 **Scrape off** the top layer of soil mix with any moss and weeds. Tease out the roots slightly with your fingers.

3 **Place the plant** in the hole, taking care not to damage the roots. Backfill with soil, firm it well, and water.

PLANTING TO THE CORRECT DEPTH

Plant most perennials, especially if in doubt, at the same depth as in their pots. Some, however, grow better with their crowns above soil level; others grow more strongly if planted deeper.

Crown is slightly above the ground

Crown is at ground level

Crown is about 1in/2cm below ground level

Crown is about 4in/10cm under ground

SHALLOW PLANTING
Recommended for Sisyrinchium striatum, pinks (Dianthus), milkweed (Asclepias), rheums, phormiums, and irises.

GROUND LEVEL
Most perennials should be planted at ground level. If planted too deeply, the base of the stems will probably rot.

BELOW GROUND
Recommended for hostas, dicentras, foxtail lilies (Eremurus), peonies, and lily-of-the-valley (Convallaria).

DEEP PLANTING
Recommended for crinum, crocosmias, monkshood (Aconitum), Solomon's seal (Polygonatum), and alstroemerias.

PLANT CARE THROUGH THE YEAR

GOOD PREPARATION and planting encourage plants to make healthy, sustained growth. Water only until established, preferably using recycled water or collected rainwater. Mulching helps suppress weeds, conserve moisture, and improve soil structure. Some perennials may need support; many can be encouraged to flower better, and some benefit from regular division (*see p.57*).

FEEDING AND WATERING

An annual application of bonemeal or general-purpose granular fertilizer in spring should provide a sufficient supply of nutrients. Keep all fertilizers off leaves, flowers, and stems to avoid scorching.

The need for watering will depend on soil and weather conditions and on the nature of the individual plants. Most established perennials grown on well-cultivated ground will need little watering (many positively thrive in dry soil), but young plants must have plenty of moisture until they are well established. To achieve maximum benefit, irrigate in early evening when the water will evaporate less quickly, and direct the water down to the roots.

Liquid feed is useful for plants in containers

Controlled-release pellets and powder fertilizers washed in by rain

Organic mulch taken in by worms and other creatures

Fertilizer added at time of planting

Organic matter dug in when preparing soil

WAYS OF FEEDING PLANTS
A careful balance of organic matter, fertilizers, and water will ensure healthy plant growth.

APPLYING DIFFERENT TYPES OF MULCH

Organic mulches help suppress weed growth, retain moisture, and, as they are gradually incorporated into the ground, will help improve soil structure.

Commercial sheet mulches made of paper or landscape fabric let water through yet make effective weed suppressors. Apply mulches when the soil is moist.

ORGANIC MULCH
Apply compost, rotted manure, or leafmold at least 1in deep. It can scorch stems, so leave the base of plants clear.

SHEET MULCHES
Special garden fabric may be used as a mulch if laid before planting. Cut crosses in the fabric to plant through.

ORNAMENTAL MULCH
Shredded bark or stone chips hide sheet mulches or provide a decorative, weed-suppressant soil covering.

PROVIDING PLANTS WITH SUPPORT

Start with as many freestanding plants as possible (*see below*) to avoid the need for staking. Support is necessary for tall perennials or for plants with fragile stems, especially in exposed areas. Insert supports early in the season – this will make the task easier and minimize damage to growth. Use stakes that are about two-thirds of the plant's eventual height, and push them firmly but carefully into the ground near the base of the shoots. Space stakes evenly around the edge of clumps. Stake guards, such as corks, are recommended to prevent accidental eye injury. Although obtrusive at first, ring or link stakes will soon be camouflaged by foliage.

RING OF STAKES
Place stakes around multi-stemmed perennials or plants with a floppy growth habit. Loop twine around the circle to support the plant.

LINK STAKES
Support tall clumps with link stakes. Insert these deep into the ground at the start of the growing season, raising them as the plant gains height.

RING STAKES
Ring stakes support clump-forming perennials. Insert the stakes deeply, then raise them as the plant grows through the support.

SINGLE STAKE
When 8–10in/20–25cm high, delphiniums and other plants with tall single stems should be staked. Use garden twine to tie the stem loosely to the cane.

WHICH PLANTS NEED SUPPORT?

FREESTANDING PERENNIALS
Many clump-forming perennials, including columbines, cimicifugas, daylilies (*Hemerocallis*), hardy geraniums, geums, and rudbeckias, do not need support. Look for (often newer) short or compact versions of slender-stemmed plants such as delphiniums and asters to cut down the need for staking.

STAKING SINGLE STEMS
Stake individual stems of monkshood (*Aconitum*), campanulas, delphiniums, sea hollies (*Eryngium*), physostegias, and verbascums.

SUPPORTING CLUMPS
Tall clumps such as astilbes, goldenrod (*Solidago*), heleniums, tall asters, and liatris may need encircling support, such as twine around stakes or link stakes (*see above*); perennials with heavy flowerheads, such as dahlias, lupines, and peonies, will benefit from the extra support of ring stakes.

COLUMBINE

IMPROVING FOLIAGE AND FLOWERING DISPLAYS

Thinning or pinching out shoots results in better flowers on certain plants. For many more, deadheading and cutting back can extend the flowering season and will prevent the plants from self-seeding. The amount of stem to be removed depends on the plant. These tasks are by no means essential, but they do result in a finer show.

BETTER FLOWERS
In spring, thin young shoots when no more than a third of their final height. Remove about one shoot in three by cutting or pinching out the weakest at the base.

Plants improved by thinning:
Aster, Delphinium, Lupinus (lupines), **Phlox, Solidago** (goldenrod)

BUSHY PLANTS
When the shoots are one-third of their final height, pinch out the top 1–1½in/2.5–4cm, just above a leaf joint. This encourages branching and bushier growth in the future.

Plants improved by pinching out:
Aster, Chrysanthemum (pinch twice), **Helenium, Phlox, Rudbeckia**

MORE FLOWERS
Remove flowerheads as they start to fade, cutting the stem back to a sideshoot (if possible). This may encourage the plant to produce another flush of flowers.

Plants that benefit from deadheading:
Chrysanthemum, Dianthus, Lupinus (lupines), **Mimulus, Penstemon, Phlox**

NEW GROWTH
Cut back old flowered stems to ground level as new shoots begin to grow from the base. This may produce a second display of flowers later in the season.

Plants that regrow well if cut back:
Anthemis, Centaurea, Delphinium, Geranium, Nepeta (catmints), **Salvia**

CLEARING AWAY MESSY GROWTH

When plants have finished their display, you can begin clearing up. Remove weeds and cut down decaying foliage and dead stems to the base. Mark the position of each plant by inserting a label in the soil. Attractive stems and seedheads (*pp.17–19*) can be left for winter, but try to clean up before vulnerable new shoots appear.

▶ CUTTING BACK BEFORE WINTER
Cut stems to ground level. Insert labels (see inset) to avoid accidentally damaging a plant before it emerges from the soil.

DIVIDING CLUMP-FORMING PERENNIALS

Division is the most reliable way of maintaining plant health and increasing stock. Most vigorous perennials (such as this sedum) will benefit from division every three to five years. Divide most plants in autumn or spring, when they will be able to reestablish successfully. Keep only the healthiest, newest sections of the original plant for replanting.

PRACTICAL TIPS

• For healthy, vigorous phlox and asters, divide established plants every year.
• A short, sharp garden knife is useful for dividing tough plant crowns.
• Divide spring-blooming plants in autumn and autumn-bloomers in spring.

Holding the roots, firmly pull the plant apart with your hands, if possible

1 **Lift the clump by** pushing a fork well under the rootball. Carefully loosen the roots by levering it up and down. Shake off surplus soil, or wash off with a hose.

2 **Divide the clump** into smaller pieces by hand or with a knife. Discard old, woody parts of the plant, retaining only vigorous portions of root with several new shoots.

DIVIDING IRISES AND BERGENIAS

Divide plants with fleshy rhizomes near the surface, such as bearded irises and bergenias, by splitting the clump into pieces by hand (for old plants you may need to undercut the clump with a spade). Cut the rhizomes into sections with a sharp knife. Plant only young sections, just covering the rhizomes and keeping the leaves upright.

1 **Having lifted** the plant, use your hands or a small knife to split the clump into manageable pieces.

2 **Using a sharp knife,** detach firm, young rhizomes, each with a shoot. Discard old, woody parts.

Trim the foliage (cut iris leaves back to about 6in/15cm). Plant shallowly, firm in well, and water.

RAISING NEW PLANTS

THE MAIN WAYS OF PROPAGATING PLANTS are by division (*see pp.56–57*), taking cuttings, and sowing seed (*see p.61*). Only division and cuttings will produce plants identical to the parent, important for named cultivars. It helps to have a cold frame, but a bright windowsill can suffice. A sharp knife or blade is essential.

HOW TO PROPAGATE BY STEM TIP CUTTINGS

A tip cutting is taken from the top of a stem just below a leaf joint. A cutting must have at least one leaf joint to root. Make sure the stem is clean before inserting into rooting medium (half sand, half peat or peat substitute), rather than garden soil. Keep the medium moist and, during the dry season, continue watering when the cuttings have rooted. The best time to take cuttings is in spring or early summer.

Leaf joint

STEM TIP CUTTING

1 **Select a short length of stem** about 2–4in/5–10cm long from the tip of a healthy, nonflowering shoot. Make the cut using a pair of pruners or garden scissors.

2 **Trim the lower end** just below a leaf joint using a sharp knife or pruners, reducing its length to 2–3in/5–7cm. Remove the lower leaves to expose a bit of stem at the base.

3 **Insert the cuttings** (about 5–6) around the edge of a 3–4in/7–10cm pot filled with rooting medium. Water, label, and cover with a plastic bag supported by stakes to keep condensation off the cuttings. Place out of direct sunlight.

Potting mix

STEM TIP CUTTINGS

SUITABLE PLANTS:
Aster
Dianthus (pinks)
Diascia
Erysimum (perennial wallflowers)
Nepeta (catmint)

Oenothera macrocarpa
Penstemon
Persicaria
Salvia (some)
Viola

4 **When the cuttings** have rooted (tap out the pot and look from after about 3 weeks), lift and pot them singly. Water in and shade them until growing well.

How to Propagate by Basal Stem Cuttings

This technique is used for perennials that produce clusters of new shoots at the base in spring. Cuttings from plants with hollow or pithy stems, such as delphiniums and lupines, as well as from plants with soft, solid stems, such as catmint (*Nepeta*) and phlox, can be rooted successfully if taken from healthy plants in midspring.

Soft stem node

BASAL CUTTING

1 **Take cuttings** when the new shoots are 2–3in/5–8cm high. Using a sharp knife, cut close to the base so that part of the woody, basal tissue is included in the cutting.

2 **Remove the lower leaves** of the cutting so that at least one node is clearly visible. Trim the lower end, making a straight, clean cut, and remove any soil from the cutting.

3 **Insert the cuttings** into a pot of rooting medium. Firm, water, and let the medium drain. Label and put the pot in a cold frame or place it on a windowsill out of direct sunlight. Cover with a plastic bag.

Insert cuttings so that the first leaf stalks are above level of medium

4 **When rooted,** lift and separate the cuttings, retaining some medium around roots. Pot individually and grow on in a cold frame or sheltered spot; plant in autumn if well grown, or wait until next spring.

BASAL CUTTINGS

SUITABLE PLANTS:
Achillea
Anaphalis
Anthemis tinctoria
Campanula
Chelone obliqua
Chrysanthemum
Delphinium
Epilobium
Galega
Heliopsis
Lysimachia
Lupinus
Lychnis
Nepeta
Physostegia virginiana
Phlox
Sidalcea
Tanacetum coccineum
Veronica

HOW TO PROPAGATE BY ROOT CUTTINGS

Root cuttings can be taken in late winter from some perennials with thick roots such as verbascums, phlox, and acanthus. It is essential to plant the cutting the right way up – making differently angled cuts will help you identify the top and bottom.

ALTERNATIVE METHOD

For thin-rooted perennials (*see box below*), lay the cuttings horizontally on moist, firmed medium. Cover with a layer of medium.

1 Lift the plant and wash the roots. Choose pencil-thick roots and cut them close to the crown. Keep all the cuttings the right way up.

2 Trim the roots smooth and cut into lengths of 2–4in/5–10cm. Make a straight cut at the upper end and an angled cut at the lower end.

3 Fill a pot with rooting medium. Insert the cuttings, straight end at the top, flush with the surface. Firm and water in.

4 Topdress the pots with coarse grit and label. Place in a cold frame or in a sheltered spot with some protective cover. Do not water until the cuttings start to grow.

5 When the cuttings have developed shoots, lift and pot up individually, using soil-based mix. Water, label, and return to the cold frame until large enough to plant out.

ROOT CUTTINGS

SUITABLE PLANTS:

Acanthus	Campanula	Eryngium	Phlox
Anemone	(lay horizontally)	Filipendula	Primula denticulata
(lay horizontally)	Echinacea	Paeonia	Pulmonaria
Brunnera	Echinops	Papaver orientale	Verbascum

GROWING PERENNIALS FROM SEED

Simple and inexpensive, raising plants from seed, especially when collected yourself, is ideal when lots of plants are required. However, few cultivars breed true, and species may vary from the norm. It usually takes a year to produce a flowering plant.

SAVING SEED

Save your own seed from perennials such as *Aquilegia, Astrantia, Campanula, Polemonium,* and *Scabiosa.*

1 Fill a tray with moist multipurpose or seed soil mix. Level it with a block of wood and firm to about ½in/1cm below the rim.

2 Sprinkle the seed over as evenly as possible. Cover with a fine layer of sieved mix. Water gently, without dislodging the seed.

3 Cover the tray with a sheet of glass or plastic to retain moisture. Put in a cold frame or sheltered place, out of direct sunlight.

4 When the seedlings have developed two pairs of leaves, transfer them into small pots. Handle seedlings by their seed leaves (the lowest pair); stems are easily damaged. Grow them on in a sheltered place out of direct sunlight (a cold frame if possible) until large enough to plant out.

Make the hole just big enough

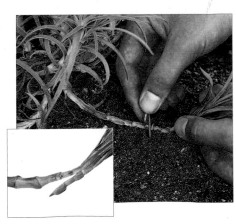

LAYERING PINKS

A few plants, most notably carnations and pinks (*Dianthus*), can be propagated by layering. Mix some peat and sharp sand into the soil around the plant. Remove all but the top 4–5 pairs of leaves on some nonflowering shoots (*as right*). Using a small, sharp knife, cut a tongue in each stem just below the lowest leaves, slicing through a leaf joint (*see inset*). Insert the cut stems into the prepared soil and pin down with a thin piece of wire. Keep the area moist until roots have formed (about 5–6 weeks), then lift the rooted layers and pot or plant out.

How to Avoid Plant Problems

PREVENTATIVE RATHER THAN REMEDIAL action will minimize the risk of pest and disease problems. A healthy plant is far less likely to succumb to attack, so start with good, vigorous stock and care for it well. Good garden management is essential, and the encouragement of beneficial insects and hand-picking of pests and diseased leaves will help. It is preferable not to use garden chemicals, which may kill indiscriminately and also often become ineffective after a while.

Creating a Healthy Garden

Good cultivation techniques, clean tools, and the inclusion of trouble-free plants (such as alchemillas, anemones, artemisias, campanulas, doronicums, geraniums, geums, lobelias, phlomis, and stachys) will do a lot to avoid pests and diseases. Always keep beds and borders clean; weeds can be a jumping-off point for pests and diseases. If you compost, remember not to add any diseased or infested material. Pick off pests and diseased leaves regularly to prevent the problem from invading the healthy parts of the plant. Grow plants such as *Anemone* × *hybrida*, campanulas, and rudbeckias, which will encourage beneficial wildlife: centipedes feed on many soil pests, ladybirds and their larvae feed on pests such as aphids (*see below*), while spiders trap a range of pests in their webs. Use chemicals only when absolutely necessary, and always ask your local garden center to recommend a suitable product.

VINE WEEVILS
Before making a purchase, and again before planting, inspect plants to find and destroy any adult vine weevils on the foliage or larvae in the soil mix.

SPIDER MITES
Most commonly a greenhouse pest, spider mites are encouraged in the garden by hot, dry summers. Regular moisture helps deter them.

APHIDS
Aphids pierce stems with their mouth parts, sucking out sap; they literally sap a plant's strength. They can also spread diseases.

A CALENDAR OF SEASONAL REMINDERS

SPRING

• Clear away any debris and remove weeds. Do not compost perennial weeds or any plant material showing signs of pests and diseases.

• Prepare soil for planting if you have not already done so. Any manure added now must be very well-rotted.

• Buy healthy plants with sturdy growth; mulch around them when planted and water them regularly.

• Feed plants with a general fertilizer or with fish meal or bonemeal.

• Stake plants that need it: be careful not to damage new growth.

• Divide or thin any overcrowded plants.

• You can take cuttings of many perennials, but they need shelter in a greenhouse or cold frame while the weather is still chilly.

• In mild springs aphids may multiply before populations of their predators, such as ladybugs, can build up. If infestations are bad, consider using an aphid-specific insecticide, or spray with insecticidal soap.

• Sow annuals to fill gaps between perennials.

SUMMER

• Pull up link and ring stakes carefully as plants gain height, and tie in tall stems to stakes.

• Water new plants before they show signs of stress due to drought.

• Apply more mulch, if necessary, to conserve moisture.

• Water plants in containers regularly, and give a liquid feed to those not supplied with slow-release fertilizer granules.

• If plants are lost to drought, consider drought-tolerant replacements such as aubretias, coreopsis, dianthus, and oenotheras.

• Cut back faded flowerheads unless you want plants to self-seed. If you wish to collect seed, leave just a few seedheads on the plant.

• Weed regularly, and keep an eye out for signs of pests and diseases.

• In dry summers, plants prone to mildew, such as phlox and asters, are especially vulnerable. Pick off leaves showing a gray-white fungal bloom. Consider spraying badly affected plants.

• Keep any cuttings you take well watered and shaded from hot sun.

AUTUMN

• Weed thoroughly.

• Plant perennials that you wish to flower in spring.

• Lift and divide overcrowded clumps of perennials.

• While the weather is still mild, autumn is an excellent time for planting perennials in well-prepared ground. Do not buy plants now, however, that like sun and light, free-draining soil: they may suffer from winter moisture when young and are best planted in spring.

• Check plants regularly for signs of pests and diseases: slugs and snails may become a problem again as the weather becomes cooler and wetter.

• Clean up beds and borders as plants fade, cutting down and removing dead stems and foliage. This will also ensure that late-flowering perennials are shown off at their best.

EARLY WINTER

• Clean up beds and borders, cutting down and removing dead growth. Insert labels where plants have died down completely, so you know where they are.

• Lift and destroy plants that have succumbed to disease.

• You can take root cuttings of many perennials now, but they need shelter from cold.

• Move perennials in containers to a sheltered spot.

• Prepare bare areas of soil for planting in spring, adding plenty of organic matter such as compost or a purchased equivalent, well-rotted manure, or leafmold. Time and frost action will help these materials break down and become well incorporated into your soil, improving its texture.

ORIENTAL POPPY

RECOMMENDED PERENNIALS

THE PERENNIALS here have symbols that indicate their preferred conditions, but many are not unduly demanding. Although many of the genera presented here are hardy (as a group) over much of North America, the hardiness of a given species often falls within only a part of that range.

☒ *Prefers full sun* ☒ *Prefers partial shade* ❊ *Tolerates full shade* ◊ *Prefers well-drained soil* ◐ *Prefers moist soil* ◕ *Prefers wet soil* **Tall** *Taller than 4ft/1.2m* **Medium** *2–4ft/60cm–1.2m* **Small** *Up to 2ft/60cm* *Hardiness zone ranges are given as* **Z** x–x

A

Acanthus (Bear's breeches)
Tall, architectural plant, with large, deeply cut leaves. Sturdy white and mauve flower spikes, borne in summer, are useful for dried winter decoration. Divide or sow seed in spring, or take root cuttings in winter.
☒ ◊ Z5–9
A. mollis p.34. Also recommended: *A. spinosus*

Achillea (Yarrow)
Forms medium-height clumps of feathery foliage. Dense, flat flowerheads appear in summer; they are long-lasting and good for drying. Divide or take basal stem cuttings in spring; sow seed in late spring or early summer.
☒ ◊ Z3–8
A. filipendula 'Gold Plate' *p.30.* Also recommended:
A. 'Coronation Gold'
A. 'Moonshine'

ACONITUM CARMICHAELII 'ARENDSII'

Aconitum (Monkshood)
Tall spires of hooded flowers in indigo blue, white, or yellow are borne in summer. Divide the tuberous roots every two years, in autumn or winter, to encourage strong stems. Sow seed in autumn. All parts are toxic.
☒ ◊ Z3–8
Recommended: *A. carmichaelii* 'Arendsii', *A.* 'Spark's Variety'

Agapanthus
Small to medium plants with erect stems, topped by round heads of blue or white tubular flowers in late summer. Strap-shaped leaves. Divide in spring. In colder areas, protect crowns in winter.
☒ ◊ Z7–10
A. campanulatus p.47.

Ajuga (Bugle)
Semi- or fully evergreen low, spreading plants, ideal as a groundcover. Some have purple or variegated foliage; all bear short flower spikes in spring/early summer. Make new plants by digging up rooted stems in early summer.
☒ ◐ Z3–9

Alchemilla mollis
(Lady's mantle)
Small to medium-sized groundcover plant with soft, circular leaves and masses of tiny, greenish yellow flowers in summer. Self-sows freely.
☒ ◊ Z4–7

◀ SPIRES AND STRIPES *Foxgloves mix with spiky sisyrinchiums and a striped lamium.*

Anemone

Wide range of tuberous or herbaceous perennials bearing cup-shaped flowers in white, blue, pink, or red. The tuberous types are often small and flower in spring; the tall, herbaceous, clump-forming Japanese anemones, such as *A. hupehensis*, flower in autumn. All anemones can be divided in autumn.
🔲 ◊ Z4–8
A. hupehensis 'Hadspen Abundance' *p.17*. Also recommended: *A.* × *hybrida* 'Honorine Jobert'

Anthemis

Carpeting or clump-forming plants with a profuse summer crop of yellow or white daisy-like flowers. The ferny foliage is sometimes evergreen. Can be short-lived. Divide in spring or take basal stem cuttings in spring or summer.
🔲 ◊ Z3–7
A. punctata subsp. *cupaniana p.28*. Also recommended: *A. tinctoria* 'E.C. Buxton'.

Aquilegia (Columbine)

Erect, small-to-medium height stems bear single and double nodding flowers in late spring and summer in many colors. Sow seed in autumn or spring. Often self-seeds.
🔲 ◊ Z3–8
A. vulgaris p.35.

Artemisia

The perennials are bushy, medium-sized evergreen or semi-evergreen foliage plants. The gray or silver fernlike leaves are often aromatic. Cut back foliage in spring. Divide in spring or autumn.
🔲 ◊ Z4–9
Recommended: *A. alba* 'Canescens', *A. ludoviciana* 'Silver Queen' (can spread).

Aruncus (Goat's beard)

Tall plumes of tiny white flowers are borne in summer above broad hummocks of fernlike foliage. Divide in spring or autumn.
🔲 ◊ Z4–8

Aster

Perennials of small to medium height with daisylike flowers. Taller ones may need staking. Sprays of small blue, violet, purple, pink, or white flowers appear mostly in late summer

AQUILEGIA 'MUNSTEAD WHITE'

ASTILBE 'APHRODITE'

and autumn and are good for cutting. Take cuttings in spring, or divide in spring or autumn.
🔲 ◊ Z4–8
A. × *frikartii* 'Mönch' *p.29*; *A. novae-belgii* 'Little Pink Beauty' *p.28*. Also recommended:
A. amellus 'King George'

Astilbe

Small to medium plants, with dense clumps of ferny foliage. Numerous red, pink, or white flower plumes appear in summer and last well when cut; dried flowerheads look attractive in winter. Can be used in waterside plantings Divide in spring or autumn.
🔲 ◊ Z4–9

Astrantia (Masterwort)

Bears unusual flowers with pink, white and green papery bracts in summer and autumn. They lend themselves to cutting and drying. Good groundcover of medium height, suitable for informal planting. Divide in spring, or sow seed in late summer.
🔲 ◊ Z4–7
Recommended: *A. major* 'Shaggy', *A. maxima*

B

Baptisia australis (False indigo)
Upright, deep-rooted plant of medium height with attractive, divided, blue-green leaves. In summer it bears erect, open spikes of small, pealike, indigo flowers. Divide or sow seed in spring.
❏ ◊ Z3–9

Bergenia
Low-growing, clump-forming evergreen valuable for its large glossy leaves, which often turn red in winter. Small, bell-shaped crimson, pink, or white flowers are borne in clusters in late winter and spring. Divide the fleshy roots after flowering.
❏ ◊ Z3–8
B. 'Silberlicht' p.38;
B. 'Baby Doll' p.28.

Brunnera
Small perennials producing open clusters of blue forget-me-not-like flowers in early spring. Leaves are large and heart-shaped. Some, such as 'Hadspen Cream', have variegated foliage that needs protection from wind. Divide in spring, or take root cuttings in mid- to late autumn.
❏ ◊ Z3–7
B. macrophylla p.38.

Buphthalmum salicifolium
Small-to-medium, upright plant producing yellow, daisy-like flowers in summer. Suitable for a wild garden but can be invasive. Divide in spring, or sow seed in late spring or early summer.
❏ ◊ Z3–7

CAMPANULA LATIFOLIA

C

Campanula (Bellflower)
Versatile range of perennials, including small rock plants and tall border species. Blue, pink, or white bell- or chalice-shaped flowers, sometimes double, are borne in summer. Leaves are often evergreen. especially if they form basal rosettes. Sow seed or take basal stem cuttings in spring, or divide in spring or autumn.
❏ ◊ Z3–8
C. glomerata 'Purple Pixie'
p.29; C. latifolia p.39;
C. latiloba p.32;
C. portenschlagiana p.47.
Also recommended:
C. lactiflora 'Loddon Anna,
C. persicifolia 'Fleur de
Neige'

Centranthus (Valerian)
Fleshy-leaved plant of medium height bearing branching heads of small red, pink, or white star-shaped flowers from late spring until autumn. Sow seed in spring or autumn. Self-seeds readily and tolerates poor conditions.
❏ ◊ Z5–8

Chrysanthemum
Useful autumn flowers that come in a wide range of colors and shapes. Spray and pompon chrysanthemums and those from the Rubellum Group make good perennials for the garden. Take basal stem cuttings in spring, or divide in early spring.
❏ ◊ Z6–9

Cimicifuga (Bugbane)
Tall, upright plant bearing slender spikes of tiny, tufted white flowers in autumn. Attractively divided leaves are mahogany-colored in some bugbanes. Divide or sow seed in spring.
❏ ◊ Z3–8
Recommended: *C. racemosa,*
C. simplex.

Convallaria majalis (Lily-of-the-valley)
Low-growing, with narrow, sometimes variegated, leaves. Small, fragrant, waxy white (occasionally pink) bells are borne in spring and early summer. Good for a shady informal border. Divide in spring or autumn.
❏ ◊ Z2–7

CIMICIFUGA SIMPLEX 'BRUNETTE'

COREOPSIS GRANDIFLORA
'BADENGOLD'

Coreopsis
Small to medium plants
bearing a profusion of yellow
daisylike flowers in summer
that are good for cutting.
Divide or sow seed in spring.
⊠ ◊ Z3–9
Recommended: *C. grandiflora*,
C. 'Moonbeam'

Corydalis
Small, low-growing perennials
with tuberous or fleshy roots
and fernlike foliage that dies
down after flowering.
Snapdragon-like blue, pinkish
purple, yellow, or white
flowers appear in spring. Can
make a good groundcover.
Divide after flowering, or sow
seed as soon as it ripens.
⊠⊠ ◊ Z5–8
Recommended: *C. flexuosa*
'China Blue', *C. solida*

Crambe cordifolia
Tall, vigorous plant with long
woody roots and big, heart-
shaped leaves. Small, white,
fragrant flowers are borne in
billowing sprays in summer.
Divide in spring, or sow seed
in spring or autumn.
⊠ ◊ Z6–9

Crocosmia
Colorful medium to tall
plants with lance-shaped
leaves. Fiery red, orange, or
yellow flower spikes appear in
late summer and early
autumn. Flowers are ideal for
cutting. Divide in spring.
⊠ ◊ Z6–9
C. × *crocosmiiflora* 'Emily
McKenzie' *p.22*;
C. 'Lucifer' *p.29*.

Cynara (Cardoon)
Tall, architectural plant
bearing large, purple, thistlelike flowerheads in late
summer. Long, silver-gray
leaves are deeply divided and
make broad clumps. Divide
plants or sow seed in spring.
⊠ ◊ Z7–9

D

Delphinium
Classic herbaceous perennials.
Plants can range from small
to tall; the large hybrids are
invaluable in summer for the
back of a border. Spikes of
single to fully double flowers
come in shades of cream,
white, lilac-pink, or
blue, often with a
differently colored,
usually dark, central
eye or "bee." The
spires need individual
staking from an early
stage. Take basal
stem cuttings or sow
seed in spring.
⊠ ◊ Z3–7

DELPHINIUM 'BLUE NILE'

DIANTHUS 'DAD'S FAVOURITE'

Dianthus (Border carnations,
pinks)
Huge range of small plants
with fragrant summer
flowers, mainly in pinks, reds,
and white, often bicolored.
Tufted foliage is often gray-
green. Make new plants by
layering or stem tip cuttings.
⊠ ◊ Z5–9
D. 'Mrs. Sinkins' *p.30*.

Diascia (Twinspur)
Small, mat-forming plants
bearing upright flower spikes
in shades of pink over a long
season. Sow seed in spring;
take stem tip cuttings in
spring or summer.
⊠ ◊ Z8–9
D. 'Salmon Supreme' *p.46*.
Also recommended:
D. rigescens, *D. vigilis*

Dicentra (Bleeding heart)
Small to medium plants, with
green or gray-green, fernlike
foliage. Sprays of heart-
shaped red, pink, and white
flowers appear in spring.
Divide in late winter.
⊠ ◊◊ Z3–9
D. spectabilis p.39. Also
recommended: *D.* 'Luxuriant',
D. 'Stuart Boothman'.

Dictamnus albus
(Burning bush)
Upright plant of medium
height, with aromatic foliage.
Heads of fragrant, white star-
shaped flowers are borne in
summer. There is a pinkish
purple variety. Resents
disturbance after planting.
Sow seed as soon as it ripens;
germination is slow.
⬛ ◊ Z3–8

Digitalis (Foxglove)
There are several biennial or
perennial foxgloves bearing
medium-to-tall spikes of pink,
pale golden brown, or lemon
flowers in summer. Divide in
spring, or sow seed in spring
or autumn.
⬛⬛ ◊ Z3–9
D. grandiflora p.39. Also
recommended: *D. ferruginea*,
D. × mertonensis

Doronicum 'Miss Mason'
Small, easily grown plant (*see
p.29*) bearing yellow daisy
flowers in mid- to late spring.
These are good for cutting.
Sow seed in spring, or divide
in autumn.
⬛ ◊ Z4–8

DIGITALIS FERRUGINEA

ECHINACEA PURPUREA
'ROBERT BLOOM'

E

Echinacea (Coneflower)
Upright, vigorous medium-
height plants, bearing large,
daisylike, red, pink, or white
flowers with domed centers in
summer. Sow seed in spring,
take root cuttings in autumn
and winter, or divide in spring
or autumn.
⬛ ◊ Z3–9

Echinops (Globe thistle)
Medium to tall, clump-
forming plants, bearing silver,
gray, or blue spherical
flowerheads in summer above
spiny, downy leaves. The
flowers dry well. Sow seed in
spring, divide in autumn, or
take root cuttings in winter.
⬛ ◊ Z3–9
E. bannaticus p.31.

Epilobium (Willow herb)
Willow herbs can be invasive.
E. angustifolium 'Album',
with medium-height spires of
white flowers in summer, is
good in a wild garden. Divide
in spring or autumn.
⬛ ◊ Z3–7

Epimedium
Small, clump-forming,
deciduous or evergreen plants,
often with coppery leaves.
Dainty white, yellow, pink, or
purple flowers appear in
spring. Clip back old foliage
in early spring for the best
display. Good groundcover.
Divide in spring or autumn.
⬛ ◊ Z4–9
Recommended:
*E. grandiflorum, E. ×
perralchicum, E. × rubrum,
E. × youngianum*.

Eryngium (Sea holly)
Thistlelike, medium or tall
plants. Round or egg-shaped,
blue or white flowerheads are
borne in summer above spiky
bracts. Excellent for drying.
Divide in spring, or take root
cuttings in winter.
⬛ ◊ Z3–9
Recommended: *E. alpinum,
E. × tripartitum*

Eupatorium purpureum
Tall, robust plant bearing
clusters of small white, pink,
or purple flowers from late
summer to autumn. Attracts
bees and butterflies. Foliage
sometimes tinted purple.
⬛ ◊ Z3–9

Euphorbia (Spurge)
There are several perennial
spurges, varying greatly in
size. Most have eye-catching
yellow-green, occasionally
flame-colored, flowerheads in
spring and summer. Foliage is
often blue-green. Sow seed or
divide in autumn, or take
basal cuttings in spring or
summer. Sap can irritate skin.
⬛ ◊ Z4–10
Recommended: *E. griffithii,
E. myrsinites, E. palustris,
E. polychroma*

EASY FERNS

Athyrium
Medium-sized, deciduous, with lacy fronds, usually green but in *A. niponicum* var. *pictum* with gray and purple tones.
❊ ◊ Z4–9

Dryopteris
Handsome, medium-sized ferns with fronds that form shuttlecocks. Usually deciduous.
❊ ◊ Z3–9
Recommended: *D. affinis, D. wallichiana*

Matteuccia struthiopteris
Deciduous, spreading fern with tall shuttlecocks of light green fronds.
❊ ◊ Z3–8

Polystichum
Mostly evergreen, medium-sized, architectural ferns with fronds fanning out in an open shuttlecock.
❊ ◊ Z3–9
Recommended:
P. aculeatum,
P. setiferum

DRYOPTERIS AFFINIS

F

Filipendula (Meadowsweet)
Tall, upright plants bearing plumes of tiny, fragrant, cream or pink flowers from late spring to late summer. Large, lobed leaves are green or gold. Divide in spring or autumn, or take root cuttings in late winter or early spring.
▣ ◊ Z3–9
Recommended: *F. purpurea, F. ulmaria* 'Aurea'

G

Gaillardia
Medium-sized plants with bright, daisylike, red, orange, or yellow flowers borne on slender but sturdy stems over long periods in summer. Cut flowers last well. Plants can be short-lived. Sow seed or divide in spring.
▣ ◊ Z3–8

Galega (Goat's rue)
Tall plants producing spires of pealike white, blue, mauve, or bicolored flowers in midsummer. Naturalize or

GAILLARDIA
'DAZZLER'

grow in informal borders. Self-seeds and can be very invasive. Divide in spring or late autumn.
▣ ◊◊ Z5–10

Geranium (Cranesbill)
Useful and easy perennials of varying sizes. Many make good groundcover. Saucer-to-star-shaped white, pink, purple, or blue flowers appear in early to late summer. Lobed leaves are also often attractive. Cut back after flowering to encourage fresh foliage and flowers. Divide or take basal cuttings in spring.
▣▣ ◊ Z4–9
G. pratense 'Plenum Caeruleum' *p.34*;
G. × *cantabrigiense* 'Biokovo' *p.47; G.* × *oxonianum p.46.*
Also recommended:
G. endressii, G. 'Johnson's Blue', *G. macrorrhizum, G.* × *magnificum, G. psilostemon*

Geum
Small, colorful plants for the front of the border with yellow, orange, or red flowers from late spring to summer. There are several to choose from; some small species are grown as rock plants. Divide in autumn or spring.
▣ ◊ Z5–9

Gypsophila (Baby's breath)
Airy clouds of tiny white or pink flowers are borne on small- to medium-sized plants in midsummer. Will trail over banks or walls. Good as cut or dried flowers. There are also some rock garden species. Sow seed in spring.
▣ ◊ Z4–9
Recommended: *G. paniculata* 'Bristol Fairy'

RECOMMENDED GRASSES

Briza (Quaking grass)
Medium-sized, with dainty spikelets rising out of blue-green tufts of leaves in summer. Divide in spring.
◫ ◊ Z4–10 *B. media p.35.*

Carex (Sedge, not a grass)
Tufts of green, gold, bronze, or striped leaves; catkinlike flowers in summer. Heights vary. Divide in spring.
◫ ◪ ◊ or ♦ Z3–9
C. pendula p.35.

Cortaderia (Pampas grass)
Tall, architectural, with silver plumes in late summer. Cover crowns with straw in winter.
◫ ◊ Z7–10

Hakonechloa macra
Small, low mounds of green and gold leaves; red autumn tints. Good in containers.
◫ ◊ Z5–9

Miscanthus
Tall, elegant, invaluable in mixed plantings or as a specimen. Some have striped leaves. Silky, late summer flowerheads can be left to decorate the winter garden. Divide in spring.
◫ ◊ Z4–9
Recommended: *M. sinensis*

Stipa
Medium to tall grasses, often with a lax but attractive

HAKONECHLOA MACRA 'AUREOLA'

habit. Sprays of oatlike or feathery flowers appear in midsummer. These are good for drying. Divide in spring.
◫ ◊ Z7–10
Recommended: *S. gigantea*

H

Helenium
Medium-sized, clump-forming plants with yellow, orange, red, and bronze daisylike flowers from summer to early autumn. Good for cutting. Divide in autumn or spring.
◫ ◊ Z4–8
H. 'Coppelia' p.30.

Helianthus (Sunflower)
Several tall perennials as well as the familiar annual type. Perennials have smaller double or single yellow flowers. Divide in spring or autumn.
◫ ◊ Z4–9
H. 'Loddon Gold' p.29.

Helleborus (Hellebore)
Small plants, highly valued for their winter and spring flowers in white, cream, pink,

purple, or green, some spotted maroon. Handsome foliage. Cut back old leaves as flowers open. Sow seed as it ripens.
◪ ◊ Z4–9
H. orientalis p.38;
H. × ericsmithii p.12.

Hemerocallis (Daylily)
Medium-height clumps of flowers in purple, orange, red, yellow, or pink, in summer. Flowers last only a day but appear in long succession. Straplike foliage is sometimes

HELLEBORUS ORIENTALIS

evergreen. Many hybrids. Divide almost any time.
◪ ◊ Z3–10

Heuchera (Coral bells)
Semievergreen or evergreen low, groundcover plants, with leaves colored green, bronze, or purple. Narrow spires of tiny white, pink, or red flowers appear in summer. Divide in autumn.
◪ ◊ Z3–8
H. micrantha 'Palace Purple' p.46.

Hosta (Plantain lily)
Low but dense clumps of large, heart-shaped leaves, often blue-green or marked with cream or gold, ideal as groundcover. Spikes of tubular flowers are a bonus in summer. Divide in early spring.
◪ ◊ Z3–8
H. 'Shade Fanfare' pp.40, 43;
H. sieboldiana p.38.

I

IRIS 'BROWN LASSO'

Iris
Very many small to tall plants with widely differing requirements. Bearded irises (*as above*) need sun and free-draining soil. They come in a wide range of colors with plenty of bicolors; some have ruffled petals. Other irises, such as *I. laevigata* and Siberian irises (*I. sibirica*), need moist soil and are useful for borders and waterside. Divide Siberian irises in late summer; bearded irises in mid- to late summer.
🔲 ◊◊ Z3–9
I. sibirica p.43.

K

Knautia macedonica
Medium-sized plants with deep crimson, pincushion-like flowers in summer. Excellent in informal plantings. Take basal cuttings or sow seed in spring.
🔲 ◊ Z5–9

Kniphofia (Red-hot poker)
Dazzling, medium to tall spikes of tubular red, orange, or yellow flowers are held well above clumps of strap-shaped leaves in summer. Mulch with straw in first winter. Divide in spring.
🔲 ◊ Z5–9
K. rooperi p.2.

L

Lamium (Deadnettle)
This useful, small, ground-cover plant bears white, pink, or purple flowers in late spring. Some have gold- or silver-splashed leaves. Divide in spring or take cuttings in early summer.
🔲 ◊ Z4–8

Leucanthemum
White or yellow daisylike flowers, sometimes quite shaggy-looking, are produced in summer on clump- or mat-forming plants. Divide or sow seed in spring or autumn.
🔲 ◊ Z5–8
L. vulgare p.35.

Liatris (Blazing star)
Summer- to autumn-flowering plants with medium to tall spikes of small, tufted, white or purple flowers. Divide in spring, or sow seed in autumn.
🔲 ◊ Z3–9

Ligularia
Large, robust, with tall heads of yellow or orange flowers in mid- to late summer. Excellent by water. Some have leaves with purple undersides. Divide in spring or autumn.
🔲🔲 ◊ Z4–8
Recommended: *L. dentata* 'Desdemona'

Linum (Flax)
Small- to medium-sized plants with yellow or blue flowers in spring and summer. Sow seed in autumn or take stem-tip cuttings in summer.
🔲 ◊ Z5–9
Recommended: *L. narbonense*

Lobelia
Perennials are quite different from annual bedding lobelias: medium-height border plants, they appreciate damp ground. Spires of red, blue, pink, or rich purple flowers are borne from late summer to midautumn. Foliage can be purplish red. Divide in spring. Dry-mulch to protect crowns in winter.
🔲 ◊ Z3–9
Recommended: *L. cardinalis*, *L.* 'Queen Victoria'

Lunaria rediviva (Honesty)
The biennial honesty is most commonly grown, but this perennial is an attractive plant of medium height with white or lilac fragrant flowers from late spring. Silvery seed pods dry well. Divide in spring or sow seed in autumn or spring.
🔲 ◊ Z6–9

LIATRIS SPICATA 'KOBOLD'

LUPINUS 'CHANDELIER'

M

Macleaya (Plume poppy)
Tall plants producing a profuse summer display of tiny, tubular, cream and coral-pink flowers in airy plumes above grayish, heart-shaped leaves. Sow seed in spring, or divide in spring or autumn.
☼ ◊ Z4–9
M. microcarpa 'Kelway's Coral Plume' *pp.32, 35.*

MONARDA 'BEAUTY OF COBHAM'

Lupinus (Lupine)
Elegant, medium-height spikes of pealike flowers in a wide range of colors appear in summer above attractively divided leaves. Many are bicolored. Will self-seed, but seedlings may not be like their parent. Take basal cuttings in midspring.
☼ ◊ Z4–9

Lychnis
Tall, upright, clump-forming plants bear white, pink, red, or purple star-shaped flowers, singly or in clusters, in summer. Divide and take basal cuttings in spring; sow seed as soon as it ripens.
☼ ◊ Z4–9
L. chalcedonica p.28.
Also recommended:
L. coronaria Alba Group

Lysimachia (Loosestrife)
Most types bear tall, upright spires of small, star-shaped flowers in summer in white or yellow. Good for informal plantings. Sow seed in spring; divide in spring or autumn.
☼ ◊ Z3–9
Recommended:
L. clethroides, L. punctata.

Malva (Mallow)
Easily grown plants of medium height bearing saucer-shaped flowers in white, pink, or blue from late spring to midautumn. Take basal cuttings in spring, or sow seed in spring or summer.
☼ ◊ Z4–8
Recommended: *M. moschata* f. *alba*

Meconopsis
Poppylike flowers, especially suitable for wildflower gardens or woodland settings. The tall, blue Himalayan types – *M. betonicifolia, M. grandis* – are less easy to grow than the small yellow or orange Welsh poppy, *M. cambrica.* Most prefer slightly acidic soil. Plants can be short-lived. Divide after flowering.
☀ ☼ ◊ Z5–8

Mimulus (Monkey flower)
There are several small hardy perennial mimulus bearing colorful snapdragon-like flowers from spring to summer. These may be white, yellow, red, or pink. Often short-lived. Divide in spring.
☼ ◊◊ Z4–10
M. cupreus 'Whitecroft Scarlet' *p.42.*

Monarda (Bee balm)
Clump-forming, medium-sized plants with densely packed heads of colorful tubular flowers from mid-summer to early autumn. Mainly shades of red, pink, and purple. Aromatic foliage; the flowers attract bees. Take basal cuttings or divide in spring, or sow seed in spring or autumn.
☼ ◊ Z3–9
Recommended: *M.* 'Beauty of Cobham', *M.* 'Cambridge Scarlet'

N

Nepeta (Catmint)
Small- to medium-sized plants bearing clusters of usually blue flowers in summer and early autumn. Good for softening border edges. Aromatic leaves are gray-green. Attractive to bees and often to cats. Cut back after first flowering to encourage a second flush. Divide in spring or autumn; take stem-tip or basal cuttings in early summer.
☼ ◊ Z3–9
Recommended: *N.* × *faassenii, N. sibirica.*

O

Oenothera
(Evening primrose)
Upright or trailing small to medium plants bear profuse but short-lived summer displays of fragrant yellow, white, or pink flowers. Divide or sow seed in spring, or take stem tip cuttings in late spring.
❂ ◊ Z3–9
Recommended: *O. fruticosa* 'Fyrverkeri'

Omphalodes (Navelwort)
Small, semievergreen or evergreen groundcover plants bearing small blue flowers in spring and early summer. Divide or sow seed in spring.
❋❂ ◊ Z6–9
O. verna p.38.
Also recommended:
O. cappadocica

P

Paeonia (Peony)
Medium-sized clumps of handsome foliage with sumptuous double or single

PAEONIA OFFICINALIS
'CRIMSON GLOBE'

flowers in white, pink, red, and rarely yellow, from late spring to early summer. May need support. Long-lived but resent disturbance. Divide in autumn or early spring, or take root cuttings in winter.
❂ ◊ Z3–8

Papaver (Poppy)
Perennials, flowering in early summer, range from the flamboyant, medium-height red, pink, or white Oriental types to the small yellow and orange alpine poppies. Divide or sow seed in spring; take root cuttings in winter.
❂ ◊ Z4–9
P. orientale p.48.

Penstemon
Medium-sized, clump-forming plants bearing spires of foxglovelike flowers in white and shades of pink, red, and purple from midsummer to autumn. Take cuttings in summer.
❂ ◊ Z3–10

Persicaria
Small to medium groundcover plants that can be invasive, with spikes of tiny white, pink, and red flowers in summer. Sow seed or take stem-tip cuttings in spring; divide in spring or autumn.
❂ ◊ Z3–9
P. bistorta 'Superba' *pp.40, 42.*

Phlomis
Small range of medium-sized perennials bearing tubular yellow or pink summer flowers in dense, circular clusters around upright stems. The seedheads are decorative in winter. Divide in spring.
❂ ◊ Z4–10
Recommended: *P. russeliana*

PHLOX PANICULATA
'GRAF ZEPPELIN'

Phlox
Many medium to tall border phlox to choose from, bearing clusters of white, pink, red, lilac, or purple, lightly fragrant flowers, generally toward late summer. Numerous small phlox are grown as rock plants. Take root cuttings in autumn.
❂ ◊ Z3–8

Phormium
Tall, architectural evergreen plants grown for their sword-like green, bronze, or striped leaves. Can be used to make focal points in a garden. Divide in spring. Protect where marginally hardy in winter by wrapping in burlap or bubble wrap.
❂ ◊ Z9–10
Recommended:
P. cookianum, P. tenax

Physostegia virginiana
Upright plant of medium height, bearing spikes of tubular white, pink, or purple flowers in summer. Good for cutting. Divide in late winter or early spring.
❂ ◊ Z4–8

Polemonium (Jacob's ladder)
Small, clump-forming plants
with clusters of usually blue,
sometimes pink or white,
flowers in spring and summer.
Divide in spring, or sow seed
in spring or autumn.
◫ ◊ Z4–9
Recommended: *P.* 'Lambrook
Mauve'

Polygonatum
(Solomon's seal)
Medium to tall arching stems
of white or cream bells in
summer suit shady borders or
woodland. Divide in spring.
❊ ◊◊ Z3–9
P. falcatum 'Variegatum' *p.38*

Primula (Primrose)
Vast range includes moisture-
loving candelabra primroses,
such as *P. japonica*, as well as
those with the more familiar
dainty flower clusters. Small,
clump-forming plants, they
are perfect in informal
settings and lightly shaded
borders. Many colors; some
have double flowers. Divide
in early autumn, or sow seed
as soon as ripe.
◫ ◊ Z3–8
P. japonica *p.42.*

PRIMULA 'MISS INDIGO'

Pulmonaria (Lungwort)
Small, spreading clumps of
silver-spotted leaves, with
blue, pink or white flowers in
spring. Leaf markings vary.
Divide in autumn; take root
cuttings in winter.
❊ ◊ Z4–8

Pulsatilla (Pasque flower)
Small, with ferny leaves and
silky purple or white flowers
in spring. Silky seedheads
follow. Must have a sunny,
sheltered, free-draining site.
Sow seed when ripe.
◫ ◊ Z4–7
P. vulgaris *p.47.*

R

Ranunculus
Apart from rock plants, one
of the best-known perennial
species is the small *R.
aconitifolius*, with dainty white
flowers on branching stems.
Divide in spring or autumn.
◫ ◊ Z3–9
Recommended: *R.
aconitifolius* 'Flore Pleno'

Rheum (Rhubarb)
Tall, imposing plants with
large, coarsely toothed and .
veined leaves. Tall plumes of
tiny, usually red or cream
flowers in early summer.
Divide in spring.
◫ ◊ Z5–9
Recommended: *R. palmatum*

Rudbeckia (Coneflower)
Medium to tall plants with
colorful, mainly yellow,
daisylike flowers in summer
and autumn. Good for
cutting. Sow seed in spring;
divide in spring or autumn.
◫ ◊◊ Z3–9
R. laciniata *p.34.*

S

Salvia (Sage)
Several hardy perennials
suiting a variety of sites, but
usually needing sun and good
drainage. Medium-height
summer spikes of flowers are
generally purple, pink, blue,
or white; leaves are aromatic.
Divide in spring.
◫ ◊ Z5–9
S. × *superba* *p.31.*

Scabiosa (Scabious)
Attractive blue, pink, lemon,
or white flowers with
pincushion centers are borne
in summer on wiry stems.
Small to medium plants.
Divide in spring or autumn.
◫ ◊ Z4–9
Recommended: *S. caucasica*
'Clive Greaves'

Schizostylis coccinea
(Kaffir lily)
Upright spikes of white, pink,
or red flowers, good for
cutting, appear late summer
to late autumn. Medium-sized
plants with strap-shaped
leaves. Divide in spring.
◫ ◊ Z7–9

SCABIOSA 'BUTTERFLY BLUE'

Sedum

Fleshy-leaved plants with clusters of small, star-shaped, usually red or pink flowers in summer and autumn. Foliage sometimes tinted purple or gray. Small- to medium-sized plants, the latter ones having a rather lax habit. Sedums also include several rock plants. Divide in spring.
⊞ ◊ Z3–10
S. 'Ruby Glow' *p.31;*
S. spectabile 'Brilliant' *p.17.*

Sidalcea (False mallow)

Medium-sized, clump-forming plants with spires of hollyhock-like pink or white flowers produced from early to late summer. These last well when cut. Divide in early spring; take basal stem cuttings in spring.
⊞ ◊ Z6–8

Sisyrinchium striatum

Fan-shaped clumps of lance-shaped evergreen leaves, striped cream in 'Aunt May', bear sturdy spikes of cream flowers in summer. Small- to medium-sized plants; there are also several small sisyrinchiums for rock

SIDALCEA 'OBERON'

SISYRINCHIUM STRIATUM 'AUNT MAY'

gardens. Divide in spring or sow seed in autumn.
⊞ ◊ Z5–9

Solidago (Goldenrod)

Medium to tall plants bearing plumes of tiny gold flowers from midsummer to autumn. The species are rather coarse and invasive and best in a wild garden, but the named hybrids are suited to borders. Divide in autumn or spring.
⊞ ◊ Z5–9
Recommended:
S. 'Goldenmosa'

Stachys

Low, spreading plants, good for groundcover or a border's edge. Lambs' ears (*S. byzantina*) is grown for its evergreen, silver, woolly leaves, and *S. macrantha* for its dense spikes of purple-pink flowers in summer. Divide or sow seed in spring.
⊞ ◊ Z4–8

Symphytum (Comfrey)

Small to medium, vigorous plants good as groundcover in wild and woodland gardens. Coarse, hairy leaves are at

SYMPHYTUM 'GOLDSMITH'

their best variegated (*as above*). Flowers, in late spring and summer, come in shades of blue, cream, pink, or purple. Divide in spring.
⊞ ◊ Z3–9
Also recommended: *S.* × *uplandicum* 'Variegatum'

T

Tanacetum

Pink or red daisy flowers of pyrethrum (*T. coccineum*) are useful in a border in early summers and make good cut flowers. White-flowered feverfew (*T. parthenium*) is good for border edges or informal plantings. There are also several small, silver-leaved rock-garden species. Sow seed or divide in spring.
⊞ ◊ Z4–9

Thalictrum (Meadow rue)

Attractive plants with delicate foliage, often blue-green, and sprays of tiny, tufted flowers. Those medium to tall in height are ideal for borders or more informal plantings. Flower colors include white, pink, mauve, and lemon.

TIARELLA TRIFOLIATA

Some prefer cool, damp sites. Sow seed or divide in spring. 🔲 ◊ ◊ Z5–9 Recommended: *T. delavayi* 'Hewitt's Double', *T. flavum* subsp. *glaucum*

Tiarella (Foam flower) Superb groundcover plants for light shade; leaves color well in autumn. Airy clusters of tiny, star-shaped, pink or white flowers are borne from spring to summer. Sow seed or divide in spring or autumn. 🔲 ◊ Z3–9 *T. wherryi p.39.* Also recommended: *T. trifoliata.*

Tradescantia (Spiderwort) Small plants with dense clumps of fleshy stems and strap-shaped leaves. Although the 3-petaled flowers, in white, pink, purple, or blue, are short-lived, they are produced in long succession. Divide in spring or autumn. 🔲 ◊ Z5–9 Recommended: *T. × andersonia* 'Isis'

Tricyrtis (Toad lily) Curious-looking funnel- or star-shaped flowers in white,

yellow, or pinkish purple, often spotted, appear in late summer and autumn on medium-sized, shade-loving plants. Divide in spring. 🔲 ☀ ◊ Z4–9 Recommended: *T. formosana*

Trollius (Globeflower) Medium-sized plants bear buttercup-like lemon or yellow flowers in spring or summer above clumps of deeply divided leaves. Needs moist soil; good in pondside plantings. Divide after flowering. 🔲 ◊ Z5–8 *T. europaeus p.43.*

V

Verbascum (Mullein) Spikes of flowers, yellow or sometimes white, purple, or pink, rise from rosettes of leaves, often gray and woolly. Height varies greatly. Sow seed or divide in spring; take root cuttings in winter. 🔲 ◊ Z4–9 *V. chaixii* 'Gainsborough' *p.30.*

VERBASCUM 'COTSWOLD QUEEN'

Verbena bonariensis Tall, wiry stems bear flattened heads of tiny, purple flowers in summer and autumn. Very effective in mixed, informal plantings. Often flowers in its first season if sown in early spring. 🔲 ◊ Z7–11

Veronica Generally small, low-growing plants bearing upright spikes of small flowers, usually in shades of blue, sometimes pink, from late spring to summer. Divide in spring or autumn; sow seed in autumn. 🔲 ◊ Z3–8 Recommended: *V. gentianoides*

Viola Delightful small plants with flowers, sometimes scented, in a wide range of colors. Deadhead to encourage more flowers; cut back in autumn to keep in shape, especially *V. cornuta*. Sow seed in spring; take stem tip cuttings in spring or late summer. 🔲 ☀ ◊ Z2–9 *V. riviniana* Purpurea Group *p.46.*

VERONICA LONGIFOLIA

INDEX

Page numbers in *italics*
indicate illustrations.

A

Acanthus 60, 65
 A. mollis 34, *34*
Achillea 65
 A. filipendulina 30, *30*, 31
Aconitum 24, 53, 65, *65*
Agapanthus 23, 65
 A. campanulatus 'Isis' 46,
 47, *47*
Ajuga 65
 A. reptans 'Atropurpurea'
 21, *21*
Alchemilla 25, 33, 62
 A. mollis 65
Alstroemeria 53
Anemone 17, 24, 62, 66
 A. × hybrida 62
annuals 11
Anthemis 66
 A. punctata subsp.
 cupaniana 28, *28*
Aquilegia 13, 14, *14*, 33, 55,
 55, 66, *66*
 A. vulgaris 34, 35, *35*
Artemisia 62, 66
Aruncus 37, 66
Asclepias 53
Aster 8, 16, *16*, 17, 19, *19*,
 66
 A. amellus 'Nocturne' 20,
 20
 A. × frikartii 16, 28, 29, *29*
 A. novi-belgii 16, 28, *28*
Astilbe 37, 66, *66*
Astrantia, 66
Athyrium 70
 A. filix-femina 34, *34*
 A. niponicum 38, *38*, 39
autumn perennials 16–17

B

Baptisia australis 6, 7
bear's breeches 65
bee balm 73

bellflower 67
Bergenia 18, 24, 37, 57, 67
 B. 'Baby Doll', 28, *28*
 B. 'Silberlicht', 38, *38*, 39
bog gardens 41
Briza media 34, 35, *35*
Brunnera 12, *12*, 24, 67
 B. macrophylla 38, *38*, 39
bugbane 67, *67*
bugle 65
bulbs 11, 12, 13, 37
Buphthalmum salicifolium 67
buying plants 52

C

calendar 63
Caltha palustris 41, *41*
Campanula 15, *15*, 24, *24*,
 32, 62, 67, *67*
 C. carpatica 21, *21*
 C. glomerata 28, 29, *29*
 C. latifolia 39, *39*
 C. latiloba 34, 35, *35*
 C. persicifolia 14
 C. portenschlagiana 46, 47,
 47
cardoon 68
carnations, border 61, 68
Carex hachijoensis 18
 C. pendula 34, 35, *35*
catmint 59, 73
Centranthus 67
Chrysanthemum 8, *8*, 17, 67
Cimicifuga 67, *67*
 C. simplex 17
climbers 10, 11
cold weather 7, 18
color 14–15, 20–25
columbine 13, 66, *66*
comfrey 76, *76*
coneflower 69, 69, 75
containers 9, 11, 44–47
Convallaria 53, 67
coral bells 71
Coreopsis 68, *68*
Corydalis 68
cottage gardens 9, 10
cranesbill 70

Crambe cordifolia 68
Crocosmia 14, 22, *22*, 53, 68
 C. 'Lucifer' 20, 21, *21*, 28, *29*
cuttings 58–60
cyclamen 37
Cynara 68

D

Dahlia 14, *14*, 23
damp areas 41–43
daylily 14, 22, 71
deadheading 27, 49, 56
Delphinium 10, 24, *24*, 55,
 59, 68, *68*
Dianthus 53, 61, 68, *68*
 D. 'Mrs. Sinkins', 30, *30*,
 31
Diascia 46, *46*, 68
Dicentra 13, 24, *24*, 53, 68
 D. spectabilis 39, *39*
Dictamnus 15
 D. albus 69
digging 51
Digitalis 69, *69*
 D. grandiflora 39, *39*
diseases 52, 62
division 57
Doronicum 13, 22, 62, 69
 D. 'Miss Mason' 28, 29,
 29
drainage, containers 45
dry places 15
Dryopteris 70, *70*

E–F

Echinacea 16, 69, *69*
Echinops 69
 E. bannaticus 31, *31*
Epilobium 69
Epimedium 69
Eremurus 53
Eryngium 15, 18, 25, 69
Eupatorium purpureum 69
Euphorbia 21, *21*, 25, *25*, 69
 E. schillingii 21
evening primrose 74
evergreens 7, 18

ferns 36, 37, 70
fertilizers 54
Filipendula 70
flax 72
foam flower 13, 77, 77
foliage 8, 21, 56
foxglove 39, 39, 69, 69

G

Gaillardia 70, 70
Galega 70
Geranium 10, 24, 44, 44, 62, 70
G. × cantabrigiense 46, 47, 47
G. × oxonianum 14, 46, 46
G. pratense 34, 34
Geum 62, 70
G. 'Borisii' 22
G. rivale 'Tangerine' 21, 21
globeflower 12, 77
globe thistle 69
goat's beard 66
goat's rue 76–77
goldenrod 16, 17, 76
grasses 9, 18, 19, 33, 35, 71
Gypsophila 70

H

Hakonechloa macra 'Aureola' 18
hardiness 7
Helenium 16, 71
H. 'Coppelia' 30, 30, 31
H. 'Moerheim Beauty' 22
Helianthus, 16, 16, 71
H. 'Loddon Gold' 28, 29, 29
Helleborus 18, 18, 24, 71, 71
H. foetidus 18
H. orientalis 12, 38, 38, 39
Hemerocallis 14, 22, 71
H. 'Condilla' 21
herbaceous borders 9, 27–31
Heuchera 71
H. micrantha 23, 46, 46
honesty 13, 72
Hosta 13, 13, 36, 36, 37, 40, 40, 53, 71

H. 'Shade Fanfare' 42, 43, 43
H. sieboldiana 38, 38, 39

I–K

informal borders 33–35
Iris 53, 57, 72, 72
I. sibirica 42, 43, 43
I. unguicularis 18
island beds 9
Jacob's ladder 75
Knautia macedonica 72
Kniphofia 14, 23, 72

L

labels 56
lady's mantle 65
Lamium 72
lavender 15, 15
layering 61
Leucanthemum 72
L. × superbum 20, 20
L. vulgare 34, 35, 35
Liatris 72, 72
Ligularia, 72
lily-of-the-valley 53, 67
Linum 72
Lobelia 23, 62, 72
loosestrife 73
Lunaria rediviva 72
lungwort 12, 75
Lupinus 13, 59, 73, 73
Lychnis 73
L. × arkwrightii 23
L. chalcedonica 28, 28
Lysimachia 73

M

Macleaya 32, 32, 73
M. microcarpa 34, 35, 35
mallow 73
mallow, false 76, 76
Malva 73
masterwort 66
Matteuccia struthiopteris 41, 41, 70
meadow rue 76–77
meadows 33

meadowsweet 70
Meconopsis 73
M. betonicifolia 20, 20
Mimulus 73
M. cupreus 42, 42
Miscanthus 19, 19, 35
mixed plantings 10–11
Monarda 23, 73, 73
monkshood 24, 53, 65, 65
mullein 77, 77
mulches 54

N–O

naturalistic planting 9, 33–35
Nepeta 14, 21, 59, 73
N. × faassenii 24
Oenothera 15, 21, 74
Omphalodes 74
O. verna 38, 38, 39

P

Paeonia 74, 74
Papaver 74
P. orientale 'Mrs. Perry' 20, 20, 21
pasque flower 75
Penstemon 8, 8, 74
peonies 14, 22, 53, 74
Persicaria 74
P. bistorta 'Superba' 42, 43, 43
pests, 49, 62
Phlomis 18, 19, 19, 62, 74
Phlox 59, 60, 74, 74
Phormium 53, 74
Physostegia 74
pinks 30, 53, 61, 68, 68
plantain lily 71
planting 45, 53
plume poppy 34, 73
Polemonium 75
Polygonatum 53, 75
P. falcatum, 38, 38, 39
Polystichum 70
P. setiferum 38, 39, 39
poppies 14, 22, 48, 74
Primula 22, 37, 75, 75
P. denticulata 24
P. japonica 41, 41, 42, 42

propagation 58–61
Pulmonaria 12, 37, 75
Pulsatilla 75
    P. vulgaris 46, 47, *47*

R

Ranunculus 75
red-hot poker 14, 72
Rheum 53, 75
    R. palmatum 23, 41, *41*
rototillers 51
Rudbeckia 15, *15*, 16, *16*, 22, 23, *23*, 33, 62, 75
    R. laciniata 34, *34*

S

Salvia 14, 75
    S. × superba 31, *31*
    S. × sylvestris 'Mainacht' 20–21
Scabiosa 75, *75*
Schizostylis coccinea 75
sea holly 25, 69
Sedum 17, *17*, 18, 76

S. 'Ruby Glow' 22, 23, 31, *31*
seed, sowing 61
shade 10, 15, 37–39
Sidalcea 76, *76*
Sisyrinchium striatum 53, 76, *76*
soil, preparation 50–51
Solidago 16, 17, 76
Solomon's seal 38, *38*, 53, 75
sowing seed 61
spring perennials 12–13
Stachys 13, 62, 76
    S. byzantina 18, 25
summer perennials 14–15
sunflower 16, 71
supports 27, 49, 55
Symphytum 76, *76*

T

Tanacetum 13, *13*, 76
Thalictrum 76–77
Thymus serpyllum 46, *46*
Tiarella 13, 39, *39*, 77, *77*
toad lily 77

Tradescantia 77
Tricyrtis 77
Trollius 12–13, 77
    T. × cultorum 'Alabaster' 20, *20*
    T. europaeus 42, 43, *43*

V

valerian 67
Verbascum 13, 60, 77, *77*
    V. chaixii 30, *30*, 31
    V. 'Helen Johnson' 24
Verbena bonariensis 77
Veronica 77, *77*
Viola 37, 77
    V. riviniana Purpurea Group 46, *46*

W–Z

watering 45, 49, 54
waterside planting 42–43
weeds 49, 50, 62
willow herb 69
winter 18–19

ACKNOWLEDGMENTS

Picture Research Sean Hunter

Special Photography Peter Anderson

Illustrations Gill Tomblin

Additional illustrations Karen Cochrane

Index Hilary Bird

DK Publishing would like to thank:
All staff at the RHS, in particular Susanne Mitchell and Barbara Haynes, at Vincent Square; Candida Frith-Macdonald for editorial assistance.

American Horticultural Society
Visit AHS at www.ahs.org or call them at 1-800-777-7931 ext 10. Membership benefits include *The American Gardener* magazine, free admission to flower shows, the free seed exchange, book services, and the Gardener's Information Service.

Photography
The publisher would like to thank the following for their kind permission to reproduce their photographs:
(key: a=above; b=below; c=center; l=left; r=right; t=top)

Garden Picture Library: Brigitte Thomas 18b; Howard Rice 12br, 23tl; J. S. Sira front cover crb, 16b, 16cra, 43tc; Steven Wooster 25tl; Sunniva Harte 12bl
John Glover: 2, 8b, 9tl, 14br, 22b, 44
Jerry Harpur: 6, 7br, 9br, 11br, 14clb, 48
Andrew Lawson: front cover cr, cla, back cover c, tr, tl, 9cra, 10b, 15tr, 23r, 32, 33br, 36, 37br
Clive Nichols: front cover r, 13tl, 15tl; Little Bowden, Berkshire 26; Tintinhull Gardens, Somerset 11tl
Planet Earth Pictures: Steve Hopkin 62br
Howard Rice: 19t, 19bl
Harry Smith Collection: 37bl